The Eagle's Claw

Christians and the IRS

by
Steve Richardson, CPA

Huntington House Publishers

Huntington House Publishers
P.O. Box 53788
Lafayette, Louisiana 70505

Library of Congress Card Catalog Number 96-77784
ISBN 1-56384-128-2

All Scripture quotations are from the
New American Standard Version,
unless otherwise noted.

Contents

Introduction

Freedom and America

This book is about the IRS, the economy, and our nation's
misguided tax and economic policies, but most of all it is about
freedom. Today, we face grave threats to the America in which we
all believe. Our economic and social problems seem to be overwhelming. These problems threaten the very fabric of our future.
Some say that the America in which our children and grandchil-
dren will live will be a sad shadow of a once great nation. I do not
believe that will prove to be true.

Cries of "freedom!" and "America!" are almost synonymous to
many people; that is why I believe America will overcome her
current crisis. We will ultimately win. Winning is more freedom
for more people. We have a rich tradition of moving onward to
greater freedoms. We have always had threats to freedom, setbacks that were serious, but America has survived.

We will survive again; I believe in our survival with all my
heart. The standard by which we should weigh all social and
political decisions can be summed up in that one word, *freedom!*
Freedom is not only a political word, it is an idea born in the very
heart of God. He wants us to be free. If God's people ask God to
make us more free, then we will be free indeed. I call this praying
to the heart of God.

The most basic truth about freedom is this: we are all free, or
none of us are free. Freedom for some, denied to others, is not
freedom at all. At best it is the illusion of freedom, an imitation
of the truth. To imitate the truth is Satan's tool—not ours. The
Church has too often become an imitator of the truth not a com-
municator of the Truth. Yes, I am going to get into some elements
of our society which pose a direct threat to freedom, and the
Church will be called upon to shoulder her fair share of the blame.

Today, the threat to freedom is most serious because it comes from within. Only twice before have we faced such an internal threat to freedom in America: once in the Civil War, a self-inflicted tragedy, and once again in the Great Depression, also a self-inflicted disaster.

Both catastrophes were caused by denying the maximum possible freedoms to all Americans. The Civil War occurred in part because the slaves were denied free access to life, liberty, or any form of happiness. To deny any person freedom exacts a high price in suffering. The lack of freedom is slavery, and slavery is the most evil and self-defeating of all sins. The Great Depression was created, in part, by the "Robber Barons" who denied free access to the economy to anyone, save only themselves.

Today's threats to freedom are real. We live in a land of economic slavery. The middle class is being economically squeezed. The ranks of the poor seem to expand. Millions of families are trapped in multigenerational cycles of poverty that seem all but unbreakable. These economic diseases affect all Americans, but black Americans have been the hardest hit.

Liberal social programs designed to help, have destroyed black families by causing the rise of single parent homes headed by women, encouraging teen-age pregnancies, as well as undermining the economy and work ethic of the traditional family unit. Traditional black family values are lost. That's not freedom! Black people, as a group, have never been prosperous in America; however, the Great Depression for black people began in 1964 with the birth of liberal social policy and has only grown worse. Like all slavery, the chains of this economic bondage must be broken.

Economic threats to freedom are not merely black-white racial issues. Our modern economy looks too much like the old economy of the "Robber Barons" where the rich get super-rich and the middle class is squeezed into ever lower standards of living. This squeeze swells the ranks of the "working poor." The American dream of a middle-class standard of living is rapidly becoming a myth.

The post–World War II era has been unique in American history in another way. Never before have American families worked so hard for the government. We work almost half the year just to pay our taxes. Half of our working hours are devoted to paying for our government's social policies; social policies that have failed! So much money gone, taken from middle-class families who need it. That's not freedom.

Federal tax policy reflects the distortions within the economy. High taxes sap the strength of the economy making us all less free. With less money, the freedom of middle-class families to influence the economy is reduced. When the economy is distorted, economic power becomes unfairly concentrated in the hands of the rich. Poor tax policy exasperates this underlying trend.

Poor tax policy also denies the economy capital, causing growth to slow to a crawl. Lately the economy is expanding for the rich but actually in reverse for the middle class. The economy is expanding and declining at the same time! We have a seriously distorted economy.

The economic might of other countries has caught up and surpassed America. Without capital, we are too weak to compete. The foreigner has come in to possess our land, buy our factories, take our jobs, and, even now, they control too much of our economy. That's not freedom! An economically secure America is more sure of her place in the world, making the world more free. Freedom is a legitimate political agenda for the Church.

The Christian Agenda

The economic and tax policies of our nation are of grave concern to Christians. We should focus on three "political" things:

1. Maximum civil liberties for all people.

2. Lower taxes for everyone so we can make our own economic decisions without the government robbing us of that privilege.

3. Equal access to a strong, vibrant economy which will grow a large and expanding middle class.

Equal access to the economy will be the premier civil rights rallying point of the twenty-first century. Lifting people out of poverty into freedom is a valid goal of the Church.

This is a political recipe for freedom! This is America as it should be, free of the shackles of ignorance and poverty. These are noble political goals, worthy of the Church. The objective of each is freedom!

The government cannot make us free. By trying, it has only made matters worse. Big government, by definition, and the resulting high taxes, makes us all less free. Government can encourage us to be free by creating situations and circumstances wherein we can make our own freedom. But, government's primary function is to protect us from external threats to freedom. Only a free people, in a free society, can protect their own liberty.

Freedom! Freedom! Freedom! I love that word. That's a God-breathed word. We all need to thank God for America having this hope of freedom. To make this hope a constant reality is a valid goal for the Church.

The Eagle's Claw: The IRS

Our excessive social spending and the dysfunctions within our economy have created the need for an aggressive and powerful federal agency, the IRS. The aggressiveness of the IRS is one of the most troubling symptoms of our distorted economy.

The eagle's claw is how I describe the IRS. The eagle, the symbol of our nation, has the most effective and dangerous weapons: razor sharp claws! Likewise, the IRS is both effective and dangerous.

In many ways the IRS is the most powerful agency of our federal government. The legal (and some not so legal) tools available to the IRS are impressive. These tools are more than adequate to give lawbreakers reason to pause and consider the consequences. Unfortunately, this formidable arsenal of weapons available to the IRS has, on occasion, been used against the innocent. Serious abuses are actually rare; however, they seem to be occurring with increasing frequency.

I believe every incident of IRS abuse relates to the adversarial antitaxpayer attitude developing within the IRS. This attitude is frightening. The immense power of the IRS is held in check by only one factor, the self-restraint of the IRS. By definition, an adversarial tax system makes enemies of citizens and the tax service. Enmity makes self-restraint less likely.

Government agencies do not have a good track record of self-restraint without close watch-dog supervision by Congress. The FBI, CIA, and other "adversarial agencies" have profited by close, careful congressional oversight. As a direct result of congressional oversight, these other agencies are now well respected. Yet, Congress has failed miserably in any efforts to oversee the IRS. Lack of congressional control and oversight has contributed to the IRS's unpleasant reputation.

The IRS's appalling reputation is, in some ways, unfair. The IRS has a federal mandate to enforce the nation's tax laws, a huge responsibility. However, Congress writes bad tax laws and, somehow, expects the IRS to make it all work out. These contradictory burdens on the IRS negate any efforts at congressional oversight. Add to these factors the immense police powers of the IRS, and the results can be devastating.

Razor sharp claws indeed! The IRS is, perhaps, the only law enforcement agency not completely under the control of our nation's government.

The IRS and the Church

The IRS's sharp claws have raked and cut the Church. The adversarial attitude, typical of federal tax dealings, is business as usual in the often hostile relationship between the IRS and the Church. In some situations this hostile atmosphere has risen to a fever pitch.

The Church/IRS relationship is growing more contentious. Ironically, in the past, the Church and the IRS have had a respectful, if hands off, attitude concerning one another. It is true that to some degree the IRS is merely reflecting the changing values of our society. However, there is much more to this anti-Christian bias than the behavior of the IRS. I see this emerging atmosphere of suspicion and hostility within the IRS as a very small part of the anti-Christian bias growing in our nation.

As I will demonstrate in this book, pervasive anti-Christian social trends have caused the IRS to aggressively scrutinize the Church. This situation is uncomfortable for both the IRS and the Church for a variety of reasons, not the least of which are the serious constitutional issues raised.

Society's Anti-Christian Bias

The current anti-Christian bias in our society is a fact. This bias causes me grave concern. I have explored the roots of this hostility and reached surprising conclusions. Based upon my research, I believe I now know how we might begin to heal the relationship between the IRS and the Church. My conclusions may also point to a possible cure for the larger problem of the increasingly bitter separation between the Church and the State.

The IRS Is Influenced by Society's Bias

The symptoms of the deteriorating relationship between the IRS and the Church are obvious. The modern IRS has no qualms about auditing Christian organizations or restricting the free expression of their ideas. They have become more aggressive in dealing with a whole litany of problems unique to churches, pastors, and Christian lay people.

The damage done to the IRS/Church relationship has not been one-sided. Among some church leaders, there is a cavalier disregard for the law. The growing tax protester movement in our nation has a strong following among a few misguided Christian people. In fact, a disproportionately large number of tax protesters seem to be "Christians." These are unpleasant facts. The IRS has been influenced by society's anti-Christian bias. But, as the above facts point out, there may be more to this story of a broken relationship than mere bias within the IRS. The Church must share the blame.

Conclusions

There is more than enough blame to pass around. Assigning blame will not bring healing. Making peace seems like a particularly good idea when the IRS's claws are unsheathed and held ready as weapons of war. The Word of God gives us caution in dealing with the IRS saying they "bear not the sword in vain" (Rom. 13:4).

I work with the IRS every day. Those IRS claws are dangerous; frankly they scare me. They should scare you too.

A study of the broken and often hostile relationship between the IRS and the Church will prove fascinating. It will also point out a pathway to peace between the IRS and the Church. We need to understand why we have a broken relationship and work hard to heal it. It is my prayer that this book will show us a path of peace and healing. Like any true patriot, I pray for peace.

Despite the IRS and the anti-Christian sentiment growing in America, we still live in the best country on earth, a nation worthy of a godly peace and healing. This is a patriot's dream, a dream born in a hope of freedom. Such dreams are also worthy goals of the Church.

CHAPTER ONE

The Eagle's Claw: The IRS

What Should We Think about the IRS

Unfortunately, the IRS is a major, if unwilling, player in the escalating war between Church and State. It is necessary for us to try and understand the IRS, also known as the Service, and the limitations it must work under. It is also important we remember that the IRS is not our enemy!

This book is not primarily about the IRS. When I discuss the IRS in this book, I will focus on public policy and occasionally on the IRS's internal policies and procedures. In places, I will be critical of the IRS. God knows they deserve it. However, my primary focus will be on trends in federal tax policies as they affect the Christian movement.

I want to make an important point: I do not believe in bashing the IRS. The IRS is as much a victim of bad tax law as the Church or any other taxpayer. They are powerful, and they are big! The IRS is a huge bureaucratic organization, but the IRS is not evil.[1] The overwhelming majority of IRS employees are decent people trying to do an important job. The IRS and its employees are committed to excellence in doing their job. Many of these employees are dedicated Christians. It is not un-Christian to work for the IRS, nor is it immoral.

We as Christians owe the IRS our respect: "respect to whom respect is due" (Rom. 13:7). We are obligated by our Scriptures to learn as much as we can about this "governing authority" (see 1 Pet. 2:13–17 and 1 Tim. 2:1–2).

The nation had its first income tax in 1862 to help pay the cost of the Civil War. This tax was struck down by the Supreme Court as unconstitutional. Our Founding Fathers did not provide in the Constitution for a direct tax on income. It was necessary to amend the Constitution before such a tax was legal.

The Sixteenth Amendment

> The Congress shall have power to lay and collect taxes on incomes, from whatever source derived, without apportionment among the several States, without regard to any census or enumerations.

It is this amendment to the Constitution of the United States, approved in 1913, that allowed Congress to create the income tax and the IRS.

Apparently our Founding Fathers feared that an income tax would allow unconstitutional invasions of privacy. The IRS can be plenty invasive. We amended our Constitution to allow this invasion of privacy. Sometimes I imagine our Founding Fathers looking into the future and seeing our modern tax system. I wonder what they would think about the IRS. Jefferson, in particular, would likely be very distressed that we would give such power to the federal government.

To counter anything you may have heard to the contrary, the Sixteenth Amendment to the Constitution is the law of the land. In the mythology created by some tax protestors, it is said that the Sixteenth Amendment was never properly approved and is therefore not a part of the Constitution. This position is ridiculous!

Any irregularities in the approval of this amendment are, to use a legal term, moot. I know this amendment is legal because the Supreme Court says it is legal. In our system of government, the Supreme Court is the final authority on constitutional matters; the Constitution gives them that right. If they say it is legal, it's legal and that settles it!

One premise of this book is that we must protect the Constitution, in particular the First Amendment. If we deny the power and rights of the Supreme Court, we in effect, deny the Constitution. Our Constitution established our legal rights as a free people. The Church must have a strong Constitution in order to protect its freedoms of religion. The Constitution, in particular the First Amendment, is too important to the Church. We cannot deny our Constitution when it becomes inconvenient. As citizens and as Christians, we must work within the constitutional framework to resolve vexing tax and legal problems. We must also respect the court as an integral part of our Constitution.

Without a vital Supreme Court, we do not have a functioning Constitution. Without our Constitution, all hope of civil liberty is lost. I am not ready to abandon that hope. Anyone who is ready to abandon our Constitution does not fully appreciate the level of liberty Christians have enjoyed in this nation for over two hundred years!

By virtue of the Sixteenth Amendment, as approved by the Supreme Court, our current income tax system is legal. Therefore, the IRS as an agency of our federal government, is also a legal democratically created institution. No such institution is above the democratic process, nor are they above the law. Perhaps more than any other agency of government, the IRS is a creature of laws.

The IRS Has Problems

In an organization as large as the IRS you will have some bad employees. Many of the IRS's public relations problems are caused by a small handful of bad employees or a few ill-considered internal policies. However, to call the IRS evil is ridiculous.

The IRS processes well over 100 million tax returns each year with very few errors. A few of these mistakes become headline news. Realistically, a few mistakes out of 100 million is not bad. The IRS is one of the most efficient organizations in government. They have a tough job. Generally speaking, they do their job well.

It is not possible for the IRS or any bureaucratic organization to be perfect. In a democratic society we have the right to demand perfection in our government's agencies, but we do not have the right to expect we will actually get it! We certainly will not get perfection from the IRS; it simply is not possible. They are, after all, human.

It Is Good to Criticize the IRS

Like any governmental entity in a democratic society, the IRS deserves intense public scrutiny and criticisms. Public scrutiny of the IRS is a democratic privilege; it is our right. Even unfair and harsh criticism of the IRS *is* healthy in our society. I will not bash the IRS in this book, but it does not bother me that other people have and will. Notice I said bashing the IRS *is* healthy. The IRS needs constant reminders that their power ultimately comes from the freely given consent of the governed. The governed is you, me, and any citizen who takes the time to vote.

The IRS, however, is a little too sensitive about public criticism. On 4 June 1991, I drafted an article about a particular IRS abuse of power to which the IRS strongly objected. The article is factually accurate, yet I got a personal letter from one of the top IRS officers in charge of field audits in our district complaining about my article. When a top IRS officer writes you a letter, that could be perceived as intimidating. When this IRS officer is in charge of audits, it is intimidating! When the IRS officials use their power and authority in an attempt to limit public debate, they violate the civil rights of all Americans. Free speech is a precious right that demands protection. Limiting free speech by intimidation is criminal.

Former Congressman George Hansen, author of *To Harass Our People,* believes he was repeatedly audited by the IRS for publishing his IRS-bashing book. If that is true and he can prove it, Mr. Hansen should sue the IRS. Such action on the part of the IRS would be a clear civil rights violation. A civil rights violation is a heinous crime. It is not merely a crime against an individual, it is a crime against everyone in our society. Frankly, it is very doubtful that Mr. Hansen could prove such a charge. In fact, there was a lot about Mr. Hansen's book I would categorize as very doubtful. However, the IRS took grave offense to his insignificant little book.

Why Is the IRS So Sensitive?

Part of the IRS's sensitivity is their belief that many of the IRS-bashing books and news headlines focus on the exceptions, the one or two bad employees out of tens of thousands or the few return processing errors out of millions of tax filings that may blow up into newspaper headlines, even the stray collection effort that results in the suicide-death of a taxpayer.[2] It is a fact that a lot of IRS-bashing books and articles are unfair.

Many times, these bash-the-IRS books are unfair. There are some books in print that paint the IRS as the agent of Satan or a part of a shadow government—a truly evil empire. Such books are ridiculous, but not unhealthy as a part of free speech and the democratic process. A note of caution however: such books often lead readers to inappropriate conclusions and to support illegal actions. If you read anti-IRS books at all, please read them intelligently as law abiding citizens.[3] Nothing you read in my book should be interpreted as encouraging to tax protestors or other lawbreakers. I cannot condone those who would violate our laws. Even so, the IRS is entirely too sensitive to bad press.

Lighten Up a Little!

When the IRS makes a mistake, they should correct the situation and publicly apologize to those involved. It would make them appear more human. Even when a high-profile case is settled and the IRS loses, they will not admit error. In my opinion, the single biggest problem with the IRS is that they generally will not admit to a mistake. At the same time, they will occasionally force taxpayers to publicly admit to their mistakes.

Many people fear the IRS as "Big Brother," the all-knowing, all-powerful, invader of privacy who routinely uses coercions and fear against honest citizens. This is a false impression with a tiny kernel of truth, enough truth to make the lie more believable. This image of the IRS is unintentionally created by the IRS itself. The IRS should clean up its image.

My advice to the IRS is lighten up a little! Enjoy the benefits of being a creature of Congress and a full partner in the democratic process. Allow, even encourage public scrutiny and oversight. Stop trying to protect Congress when they write dumb laws. Encourage taxpayers to take their problems with the law directly to Congress.

The IRS has actually asked for my advice a number of times in various professional forums and meetings where IRS representatives are invited to participate. They've asked for my advice, but, as near as I can tell, the IRS has never taken my advice seriously. When informed citizens offer advice, the IRS should seriously consider it and act upon it when appropriate.

Any effort to hide or shield the IRS from the democratic process will have a predicable and unpleasant effect: in the minds of Americans, the IRS will look more and more like the "Secret Police." Americans will tolerate this image of the IRS for only a little while. Unless the IRS works to moderate its image, we will have a grassroots taxpayer revolt. A nationwide tax revolt would have unimaginable tragic consequences.

Our nation has sharply changed its political direction more than once. America's ballot-box revolutions have one thing in common—they all involve fiscal and tax policy.[4] Politicians and bureaucrats who ignore America's turbulent political history may find themselves victims of yet another voter revolution.

The Limited Power of the IRS

The power of the IRS is immense, and it grows more powerful daily. The IRS grows stronger with every exercise of their police and judicial powers. If for no other reason we must respect the IRS. Power demands our respect. Additionally, Scripture demands we respect the IRS.

Many people believe that the IRS is the most powerful human institution on earth. Few things strike fear into the hearts of Americans like the IRS. There are good reasons to fear the IRS; however, the IRS is not nearly as powerful as most people believe. These exaggerated fears of the IRS are due to a lack of knowledge.

If a man takes a gun and commits murder do we put the gun on trial? Of course not! The gun is a slave to whomever uses it. The IRS is like that gun.

The IRS Is a Slave!

The IRS is a slave to Congress. In the most simple terms, Congress writes the tax law, and the IRS is asked to enforce the law. The IRS is bound by the statute. This is a very real restriction on the power of the IRS. The IRS works the will of its master: Congress.

It is true that the IRS has substantial input into the legislative process. They advise Congress on new tax laws, make recommendations, and often draft proposed legislation for Congress. It is also true that the IRS does not always get its way where Congress is concerned. The IRS routinely suffers legislative setbacks at the hands of Congress. In fact, Congress has often passed bad laws over the objections of the IRS.

In general, the attitude of the IRS is that their job is to enforce and obey the law. What the IRS likes or dislikes about the tax law is, to them, irrelevant. If they do not like a new law, the position of the IRS is, simply, "it's a dirty job, but somebody's got to do it." They will work to change bad law. In fact, sometimes the IRS will show more *grace* in administering law than Congress actually allows in the statute. However, the IRS will actively enforce bad law even as they try to change it. They're cops. What choice do they have?

The IRS is powerful, but think how limiting it is to be a creature made by and controlled by Congress. The IRS deserves our fear. They are a powerful and fearsome weapon, like the eagle's claw. It is also certain that the IRS deserves our respect for doing a very difficult job and, generally speaking, doing it well.

When the Slave Becomes the Master

Congress issued a severe reprimand to the IRS in the Tax Reform Act of 1984. In this act, Section 1052, ministers were guaranteed a tax deduction for interest paid on their homes, but the position of the IRS was that ministers were not entitled to this tax deduction.[5] Congress revoked the IRS's Revenue Ruling (Rev Ruls) and issued the IRS a reprimand for exceeding its authority. In this situation, the IRS tried to legislate (create) new law, but creating new law is the function of Congress. Congress can get irritable when their authority is usurped by a mere governmental agency.

Conversely, Congress recognizes that it often writes bad tax law and therefore directs the IRS to correct the law through regulations and rulings. The IRS is the most dangerous when it creates new law, and it does so routinely through Rev Ruls and Regulations. Rarely does Congress reprimand the IRS for this sort of legislative activity even though such rules lack the normal due process of legislation.

Regulations requested by Congress are called Statutory Regs and have the force and effect of law unless shown to be in conflict with the law. To show that a regulation violates the law you must go to court. The IRS is sued many times every day, and it does not have a good track record in court. In fact, the IRS only wins 46 percent of its tax cases.

When the IRS legislates new law, it makes mistakes.

The IRS Makes Mistakes, Huge Mistakes

It is true, the IRS does make mistakes. An IRS mistake is an honest error made in attempting to administer complex tax law. To hear the IRS's spokespeople talk, you get the impression that they believe the IRS is perfect. This public representation is so false that it only aggravates citizens. In books and press about the IRS, you often hear terms like *arrogant* applied to the tax service.

You would think they could hire a good public relations firm. It is a truism that the IRS does make mistakes, and they should admit to their mistakes when they occur. Admitting to an occasional error would actually help the IRS's public image.

But, listen carefully, unless you consider IRS enforcement of bad tax law a mistake, the IRS actually makes very few mistakes. At least from the perspective of the IRS, administering bad tax law is not really a mistake.

The IRS Is Often Wrong

Being asked by Congress to administer a tax law that is unfair or damaging to the economy is wrong. Worse yet, being asked to enforce a law that is unconstitutional is outrageous. It is a wrong done to citizen-taxpayers, and it is a wrong done to the IRS.

The IRS often takes action that is downright wrong, even immoral, and certainly abusive. The IRS has driven citizens to depression and to suicide. I have personally seen the IRS ruin a good citizen without a good reason to do so. In my opinion, the IRS cannot be blamed for these situations. The IRS is not responsible; it, like a gun, is merely a tool.

The Unrestricted Power to Audit

The power of the arbitrary audit, the possibilities of intimidation over filing details and judgment factors, and the required waiver of Fifth Amendment rights, make the IRS, if used wrongfully, the most dangerous threat of destructive cancer to our system of self-government and our individual rights and freedom.

The IRS must be totally objective, colorblind, nonpolitical, and religiously and philosophically neutral. The virtual impossibility of your task makes your challenge great and the consequences of your failure a "hell" for the victims.

The implied threat of an IRS audit is often enough to frighten honest folks into agreeing with the IRS, even when the IRS is wrong. I had a case where a traveling salesman, out of fear, paid the tax on forty-seven thousand dollars of legitimate travel expenses that were provable. Threats and coercion should not be used to manipulate taxpayers.

Litigation

The IRS has virtually an inexhaustible amount of money to spend on litigation, and it uses this as a weapon against taxpayers who can't afford to go to court. This is called rich man's justice. Poor people already know that the courts are biased in favor of people who can afford the best lawyers. When it comes to tax lawsuits, we are all poor compared to the IRS. The IRS often goes to court when it knows it can't win merely to make an example of a taxpayer.

Two things would change this IRS behavior for the better. First, the IRS should make every effort to avoid the courts and reach out-of-court compromises and settlements. Using the mere threat of expensive litigation to intimidate taxpayers is wrong, and it certainly does not help to build a positive public image of the IRS. Second, should the IRS lose in court, they should, in every case as a matter of law, be required to pay all of the costs of litigation to the taxpayer. We need laws to dampen the IRS's enthusiasm for litigation and shut off the unlimited flow of money for antitaxpayer litigation.

IRS Collections

The legal power behind IRS collections efforts is overwhelming. The IRS can seize your property; they can garnish 100 percent of your paycheck; and, money can be drained directly out of your checking and savings accounts—even retirement savings accounts. There is very little legal restriction on IRS collections activities. If you are in business, the IRS can even direct that money owed to you by your customers be paid to the IRS. The best advice I can give any taxpayer about IRS collections is this: try not to owe the IRS any money. Pay all your taxes fairly, accurately, and on time.

I also advise taxpayers to respond to all mail from the IRS. Answer every question accurately and promptly. If the IRS seems to be sending you the same letter over and over again, keep answering it. If the IRS letter lists a telephone number to call, use it to talk to somebody with the IRS. IRS human personnel are generally very helpful. However, the little gremlins that read the IRS's mail are a different sort entirely; they are often very frustrating.

Furthermore, if you do owe the IRS money, cooperate with the collections officers. Tell them the truth, the whole truth. Never withhold information from an IRS collections officer. Collections officers are trained to help taxpayers sort out taxpaying difficulties. I have never heard an IRS collections officer give a taxpayer bad advice. But, I have seen them put a few taxpayers out of business for being less than truthful. And, finally, if you make a commitment to the IRS to make payments, keep your promise.

I have heard all sorts of horror stories about abusive IRS collections tactics. Easily 99 percent of all horror stories about IRS collection abuses will be because one of these three suggestions were violated. Some stories of abusive IRS collections activities are legendary, and most of these may be apocryphal.

To be honest, I've never experienced collections abuse against any of my clients. Quite the opposite, I have found IRS collections people, called revenue agents and revenue officers, to be totally professional. They have a job to do: collect money. What an unpleasant job! With a job like that, you can count on problems.

Even with this high level of professionalism, I believe the IRS has too much legal power in collections. To use raw power and fear as a part of public policy in a democratic society is wrong. This is not an IRS problem; it is a legislative problem. We, as citizens, need to correct this legislative problem in Congress.

The IRS is truly a slave to Congress. When the IRS takes routine actions that are clearly wrong or inappropriate, blame Congress. A slave serves its master. When the IRS spins out of control, Congress is behind the wheel, driving like a drunken fool.

If Congress says to crack down on nonprofit organizations, the IRS will comply. They may not like it, but the master calls the shots. That master is Congress; they deserve the blame. Voters should see that blame falls appropriately.

We need to be critical of the IRS. Much can be done to improve this creature of our government. However, let's reserve our harshest criticisms for the Congress who created a legal Frankenstein and forgot how to control it.

The Latest Nasty Job the IRS Really Doesn't Want

Congress is now asking the IRS to do the nastiest job in the history of tax law. This job has nothing to do with revenues and expenses, but deals with regulating and restricting the content of free speech. The IRS doesn't want this job. However, congressional pressure on the IRS to limit the political activities of ministries is intense.

Constitutional conflicts and religion are two areas the IRS has traditionally shied away from. For good reason too; these are potentially explosive issues that could seriously cripple the service's ability to administer a self-assessing tax system. The IRS is too important for Congress to jeopardize by this self-abuse.

Any effort by Congress to use the IRS as a political tool to circumvent the First Amendment will prove disastrous. It could even spark a tragic nationwide tax protestor movement.

To use the IRS as a tool to shut the Church out of the democratic process, in any way whatsoever, will have a predictable effect; the Church will be forced into political action on a scale heretofore unimaginable. We will see a voter-led, ballot-box revolution larger than any in our history. The Church can and should participate, even lead, in such a revolution. However, if we are to be a party to political efforts to reform the IRS, we must be equally active in shutting down illegal tax protestor movements. We can begin by denying tax protestor movements any claim to Christian legitimacy.

Americans, in general, and the Church, in particular, do not take kindly to any threats to our freedoms. Americans have fought and died to protect threatened freedoms in the past. Compared to such sacrifice, a ballot-box revolution is a mild response to this new threat. This voter-led, ballot-box revolution is already beginning

We do not need to de-claw the eagle. The eagle must remain strong to keep us all free. However, the eagle needs to be more responsible for its use of those terrible IRS claws, especially when those claws are turned against law-abiding citizens.

Our greatest threat to America's freedom today is our own government and its misguided tax, economic, and fiscal policies. It is only the self-restraint of a powerful federal government that keeps freedom alive in America. Unfortunately, our political leaders seem all but incapable of fiscal restraint. This lack of governmental restraint is one step down a political road we dare not travel. It is a road that leads to the systematic death of American's freedoms, one by one. Economic chaos is the death of freedom. As citizens we can provide that much needed self-restraint at the ballot box.

Endnotes

1. According to the 30 September 1992 *Semiannual Report to Congress by the Office of the Inspector General,* the IRS employs 117,950 people. The 1992 annual budget of the IRS is $7.1 billion.

2. In the *Washington Times,* 29 April 1996, Dan Gifford reported on the suicide of Mr. Alex Council which was prompted by the illegal actions of the IRS.

3. Two of the best IRS-bashing books now in print are *To Harass Our People* by George Hansen (Washington: Positive Publications, 1984) and *A Law Unto Itself, the IRS and the Abuse of Power* by David Burnham (New York: Random House Vintage Books, 1989).

4. The first such revolution in the newly formed United States of America was the Whiskey Rebellion during George Washington's administration. Another was the populist revolution which sparked William Jennings Bryant and the famous "Cross of Gold" speech.

5. On 6 January 1983 the IRS issued Rev Rul 83-3 which took the position that a minister could not deduct interest paid on his home if the minister also received a nontaxable housing allowance.

CHAPTER TWO

Comes the Wrath of God

A Nation under God

The soul of America is freedom. Our nation was founded on dreams of liberty. There is no more sacred way to make a nation. In this way alone we are perhaps still a nation under God. It is freedom which makes us a sacred nation.

America is a beacon of hope to all the people of the world. Our beloved land is proof that individual freedom is more than a dream; it can be a reality. People look to our nation as proof that freedom works. Individual freedom brings with it economic prosperity, equality, justice, and, above all else, hope.

It is threats to freedom which concern me. There are powerful social and economic forces at work in our nation that threaten freedom. Our nation's lack of fiscal restraint threatens to destroy the economy. Poverty is a road to slavery, not to freedom. If our economy begins to fail, we may have an IRS that is out of control and worse tax laws. Our methods of taxation and enforcement of our tax laws itself could become grave threats to all Americans.

I am a patriot. I love my country. In spite of our obvious problems, our nation is good. Our foundation in freedom makes us good. We have not yet abandoned this dream of freedom; I believe we never will. We can't; it's in our soul. We are Americans. That makes us special. Sure we have threats to freedom; we have always had threats to freedom, yet we are still free. I believe America will always remain free.

We cannot deny that our nation is having serious social and economic problems. We have denied God; therefore, God has

allowed us to substitute our willfulness for His will and our ignorance for His wisdom. When God allows a nation to substitute
man's limited knowledge for His divine wisdom, nations fall. Our
nation's problems may simply be God allowing us to work things
out on our own.

Nations, like men, have free will. The Old Testament calls
this dangerous state of affairs "The Wrath of God." (Ps. 78:31)
This is an extraordinarily dangerous time for every American. Yet,
we still have good reasons for hope.

I believe in the American people: we are a tough, resilient, and
creative people. I also believe America is unique. Our bedrock
principle, indeed our very foundation as a nation, can be summa-
rized in one godly word, *freedom*. Freedom is an American dream
that God can honor. God respects even the dim hope of freedom
because Christ came to set all men free. Freedom is near to the
heart of God; when we embrace freedom, we embrace something
godly.

In every other way we have perhaps abandoned God. Yet, due
to our heritage of freedom, I do not believe God will ever completely abandon us. Yes, we have problems, big problems. These
problems may get much worse; however, so long as we do not
abandon freedom, America will heal. We have good reasons for
optimism.

To Wage War upon Ourselves

America has now entered a new stage of a bitter internal war:
constitutional freedoms of speech and religion seem to be under
direct attack by our own government. Our own society seems
determined to limit the free expressions of our faith. These attacks
upon freedom are becoming more extreme. At some point in our
future, I expect the attacks upon religious freedoms to become
more vicious as they turn violent.

If these freedoms are limited, we will lose America. Any government-supported effort to weaken the First Amendment threatens to undermine the entire Constitution. Freedoms are like dominos; either they all stand or they all fall. If we ever abandon
freedom, the results will be catastrophic beyond belief.

This war, like the wrath of God, is real. It has been going on for over thirty years. I count the massive expansion of government-sponsored social programs in the early 1960s as the beginning of the war we now wage. One of the major casualties of this protracted war is the damage done to our economy by deficit spending and high taxes. This war against the Church is not merely a conflict of social ideals—we are suffering grave economic consequences. We are a nation under economic attack by our own government.

Our nation seems to wage war with itself on two fronts: our economy and our liberties are both under siege. If we lose either, the hope that is America will perish.

The ramifications of this war are almost beyond comprehension. The nearest historical parallels I can find are the judgments of God upon his chosen people, the Jews, in the Old Testament. The wrath of God is a terrifying thing for any nation to endure.

The Cause of This War Is a Failure of Hope

I would love to preach a message that those forces in our society arrayed against the Church are responsible for this tragic war. However, I am compelled to tell the truth. The real culprit in this war is us, the Church. We have allowed the social ills that plague our nation to grow out of control: violence, the breakdown and failure of public education, illegitimate births and poverty, abortion, and, above all else, racial problems. Unchecked, these social diseases will destroy America. The economy will collapse, and liberty will die. Ironically, the first freedoms we are likely to lose are now under attack, the two freedoms of religion and speech.

God Called the Church to Protect America

Losing either the freedoms of religion or speech will destroy America forever. The idea that the Church may be the primary agent of this destruction is tragic. God called us to protect America. We have failed.

Much like God gave His children, Israel, their own land, God has given to the Church a wonderful country, America! We have enjoyed unprecedented freedoms of religion in America.

God told the Jews how to protect their land. When the people of Israel followed God, their land prospered. When they refused to follow God, judgment and the wrath of God fell upon them and their nation. God is patient and merciful, but He has also given us clear instructions on how to protect our land as well. The Church has not followed God.

The failure of the Church to fulfill its God-given mission of giving hope to hopeless people in America is the root cause of this war. The crisis between Church and State is the heart of the conflict. Our government and our society, throughout America's history, have expected the Church to fulfill an active role in ministering to the nation's social needs. They have often been sadly disappointed. We have failed. In our failure lay the roots of war.

A War of Survival

Make no mistake. America is at war with herself. Deficit spending and high taxation rob our economy of prosperity. We are fighting an economic war for our survival as a free people. This war may well trigger the collapse of our economy.[1] Former U.S. Sen. Warren B. Rudman says we are fighting a war that may destroy the future of the American way of life. Such is the wrath of God.

Our nation's leaders have spent us to the brink of bankruptcy:

Presidents:	Deficit Spending (in Billions):	Federal Debt (in Billions):
Lyndon Johnson	$44.8	$493.5
Richard Nixon	$67.0	$560.5
Gerald Ford	$126.9	$687.4
Jimmy Carter	$226.9	$914.3
Ronald Reagan	$1,340.0	$2,254.3
George Bush	$1,040.0	$3,294.3
Bill Clinton, projected	$3,265.7	$6,560.0
Projected debt level in the year 2000	$6,460.9	$13,020.9[2]

The ramifications of this debt level stagger the mind. Before the turn of the century, income tax revenues will be insufficient to pay the interest on the nation's debt. This level of debt chokes off economic growth.

The problems of high taxes and aggressive tax policies pale in comparison to this staggering national debt. It is inevitable that the IRS will become more powerful and aggressive as our government scrambles to fund the nation's debt. Deficit spending and high taxes will continue to sap the economy of strength. Ever higher tax rates will continually shrink the tax base creating the cycle of economic destruction. The IRS will, unwillingly, become a central player in this unfortunate internal struggle.

Our economy is already seriously unbalanced. Our richest citizens grow superrich as the middle class slips into poverty. The contrast between the rich and the poor grows more extreme daily and will destabilize our economy even further. Our economy will crumble into bankruptcy unless something is done soon to reverse this extreme disparity between rich and poor.

If our economy does collapse in this self-defeating cycle, the ultimate casualty of this war will be freedom, the hope of every American. People in poverty cannot be free. In a time of economic collapse, freedom will be the first birthright lost. We are already deep into this slow process of losing our freedom! Already we live in fear for ourselves and our children. Our society, once so safe, is failing. Poverty destroys freedom.

People in Poverty Cannot Be Free

Poverty, born of economic failure, is the most powerful cause of modern slavery. Poverty contributes to nearly every social problem that plagues us. The primary function of the economy is to provide an adequate standard of living for a nation's citizens.

In the most important manner imaginable, the economy grows weaker daily. America's economy is squeezing the middle class. As the middle class shrinks, poverty grows. The rich grow richer while the middle class slides into despair. We are becoming a Third World country with a third rate economy. America could become a nation dominated by the superwealthy—the old Robber Barons reborn. What of the rest of us? Financial catastrophe alone threatens to overwhelm us.

A People with No Hope

Without hope, freedom is an illusion. The most basic function of government is to give its citizens hope. A failing nation is one that denies its people hope. To destroy hope is to destroy all belief in a better future. A free people must have hope in the future.

A shortage of good jobs contributes directly to the unrestrained violence on our streets and in our schools. Violence and poverty are not merely black-white racial issues. A man or a woman without a good job has a family sliding into poverty; black or white is irrelevant. When a family slides into poverty due to inadequate job opportunities, race becomes even less relevant. America's growing hopelessness adversely affects every aspect of our life, contributing to our educational failings and degraded morality.

Oppression destroys hope. The oppressions of poverty, ignorance, violence, and greed all work to destroy the spirit of freedom in the souls of people. A people without hope easily falls into slavery. Freedom and slavery cannot exist side by side together in America. At best, one group will have the illusion of freedom, but never the reality.

The Grace of God

I believe the Church can still offer hope and freedom to our nation. I believe our success or failure as a nation depends upon us, the Church of our Lord. If we fail, our nation will fail. The promises of God are clear: "If My people, who are called by My name, shall humble themselves and pray, . . . I . . . will heal their land" (2 Chron. 7:14). The prayer of my heart is for God to heal our land. It is apparent to me that our only hope for healing is in God's grace.

The grace to heal a nation is specifically given to the people called by the name of the Lord, Christians. God, for whatever reason, has chosen to give authority to hold or loosen His grace upon our nation to us, the Church. The healing begins when we humble ourselves and pray. To be humble we must recognize how we have failed our nation. We must understand our enemies and love them. We must know why our enemies hate us (see 1 Pet. 4:4).

We are the redeemed Church of a holy God, but we are far from perfect. We are, after all, merely human. If we are humble, however, we can learn. God has much to teach us. We can also learn from the people who may even hate us. First Peter 5:6 exhorts believers, "Humble yourselves therefore under the mighty hand of God, that He may exalt you in due time." To learn from people who hate us will require more humility than we are likely to have without God's help, but God has promised His help.

As a nation we have stumbled blindly into the wrath of God. Only a holy Church can lead us back to the promised land of freedom. Freedom is a sacred goal for our nation and our Church. It is the path by which we can return to God.

Endnotes

1. Larry Burkett has written extensively about this possibility. I recommend his book *The Coming Economic Earthquake* (Chicago: Moody Press, 1991). An excellent secular book on the topic is *Bankruptcy 1995, The Coming Collapse of America and How to Stop It,* by Harry E. Figgie, Jr. (Boston: Bay Back Book, 1993).

2. Grace Commission data.

CHAPTER THREE

Taxation: The Wrath of God

The late Baptist evangelist B.B. Caldwell made the following prediction in a sermon entitled "Seven World-Shaking Events Soon to Come to Pass":

> I predict that the final oppression of Christianity will start with taxation. There will be universal taxation of the Church. This will start with a series of independent churches and missionary associations, thereby casting a shadow upon their integrity and raising doubts in the minds of contributors as to the validity of their ministries. The government will haul ministers of the Gospel into court on alleged tax irregularities and challenge ministerial authority of independent ministers of the Gospel. The government will get rid of independent ministers, churches, and associations leaving only IRS approved Churches. A state approved church will become inevitable.[1]

This sermon was preached long before taxation of the Church and other Christian organizations became a hot topic. It is indisputable: taxation is a powerful weapon of the State. Chief Justice John Marshall, as a part of a precedent-setting tax case before the Supreme Court, once said, "The power to tax is the power to destroy."[2]

The Casualties of War

Every day that I go to work I experience some new crisis or casualty in this bitter war between Church and State. This book will chronicle some of my experiences defending the Church from attack in this war. I will look at many of the weapons of attack and methods used defending the Church. Our current crisis is more than a conflict between Church and State; at times, society itself seems to wage war against the Church.

It upsets me to be forced to fight in a war that can have no winners, only losers. Unless we can change the direction our nation is heading, we will have a time of hardship and chaos modern Americans cannot comprehend. America has never experienced the unbridled wrath of God. I believe God is telling us how to prevent this tragedy in the pages of the Bible.

The Wrath of God Often Involved Heavy Taxation

The Jewish people knew times of faith and saw the miraculous provision of God for their nation. These times of godly faith were also times of peace and economic prosperity. However, the children of Israel did not often obey God. The results of disobedience to God were catastrophic! We should work hard to avoid the judgment of God.

Early in Jewish history God made it clear that He would use unfriendly governments and punitive taxation as judgments upon the children of Israel for their disobedience (see 2 Kings 23: 33–37). In times of God's judgment, taxation was so high it ruined the Jewish economy. Slavery, poverty, ignorance, and greed seem to follow after God's judgment.

Punitive Taxation

Judah's exile into Babylon is another example of God's judgment upon a disobedient people. The temple was robbed, then destroyed, and their priests were carried captive into slavery.[3]

The peace of Jerusalem was brutally shattered by Babylon. Captive for seventy years and defenseless without a city wall for an additional eighty-two years, the Jewish people were forever changed by these events. God loves these people more than we can comprehend, yet He allowed His chosen people, the Hebrew nation, to endure war, slavery, poverty, and fear. God did not cause these people to suffer. Disobedience to God's Word caused the destruction of the Jewish nation.

As a defeated people, the Jewish nation was led into Babylon in 597 B.C., where they would remain captive for seventy years.

When released, only a small, faithful remnant chose to return to Jerusalem with Ezra. Ezra records an incident where the local, non-Jewish peoples used taxation as a weapon in an effort to stop God's work (Ezra 4:13). As part of the restoration of Jerusalem, Ezra planned to rebuild the walls of the city but was prevented by this implied tax threat. Eighty-two additional years passed before Nehemiah could lead the people to rebuild Jerusalem's defensive walls (see Neh. 6:15).

After a cruel seventy years of captivity, God again showed the people how obedience to God provides protection against punitive taxes. Ezra, a man who tried diligently to follow God, demonstrated such protection (see Ezra 7:24). When God's laws are obeyed, the priests and places of worship are protected from punitive taxation.

When a Nation Abandons God

The phrase "did evil in the sight of the LORD" leaps off of the pages of the Old Testament. Repeatedly in Scripture, God led His chosen people, the Jews, to a renewal of their faith. Again and again, the Jewish people abandoned God's Word. The Jewish people did evil in lusting after false gods: Baal, Ashtaroth, Molech, among others.[4]

The Hebrew people also abandoned the ethical teaching of their Scriptures. They were told to live morally and ethically, to treat their workers well, break the "Yokes of Oppression" that make men slaves: to provide food, clothing, and shelter for the poor, and to care for the needs of their own families (see Isa. 58:6–7).

Isaiah 58:6–7, New American Standard	My own paraphrase
Is this not the fast which I chose, to loosen the bonds of wickedness, to undo the bands of the yoke, and to let the oppressed go free,	This is true religion: Live as a people who love justice. Eliminate those things which make men slaves and work to set men free: Remove poverty, ignorance and greed.
and break every yoke?	
Is it not to share your bread with the hungry, and bring the homeless poor into the house; when you see the naked, to cover him, and not to hide yourself from your own flesh?	Feed the hungry. House the homeless. Clothe the poor. Care for your own family's needs.

When these special people followed God, they knew the peace of walking in God's will. Somewhere in the practice of their religion, they lost God. When the Jewish people were evil, God no longer took delight in the worship of His people (Isa. 1:11–17). The faith of the Jewish people became merely rituals and traditions which only served to cover their wickedness (see Isa. 58:3–4 and Mic. 6:8). God promised the Jewish people judgment if His teachings were forsaken, but God also promised forgiveness and healing to His people.

A proud, arrogant people cannot know God. Only a humble people who know God can heal their land.

God's Requirements of His People Have Not Changed

God has promised to bless us and our land if we will keep His commandments. And, God's standards for acceptable worship for the Jews in the Old Testament and for us, the New Testament Church, are remarkably alike.

> Pure religion and undefiled before God and the Father is this, To visit the fatherless and widows in their affliction, and to keep himself unspotted from the world. (James 1:27)

> For I was hungry, and ye gave me food; I was thirsty, and ye gave me drink; I was a stranger, and ye took me in. (Matt. 25:35)

> If a brother or sister be naked, and destitute of daily food, And one of you say unto them, "Depart in peace, be ye warmed and filled"; notwithstanding ye give them not those things which are needful to the body, what does it profit? (James 2:15–16)

> But whoso hath this world's good, and sees his brother in need, and shutteth up his bowels of compassion from him, how dwelleth the love of God in him? My little children, let us not love in word, neither in tongue; but in deed and in truth. (1 John 3:17–18)

> But if any provide not for his own, and specially for those of his own house, he hath denied the faith, and is worse than an infidel. (1 Tim. 5:8)

If we fail to keep God's commandments, He has promised judgment to correct our behavior (Heb. 12:5–7). Like the Jewish people, the price of disobedience is high (see 2 Tim. 3:1–5). The very fabric of our society will begin to breakdown. Reading 2 Tim. 3:1–5 sounds too much like the country in which I already live! This scares me. The price of our failure will be the loss of America.

What's Obedience to God Got to Do with Taxation Anyway?

Tax exemption is a privilege granted by our government in recognition of the benefits an organization gives to our society. The privilege is granted because such an organization lessens the "burdens of government."

The idea that an organization should be blessed by the government because it "lessens the burdens of government" is as old as ancient English common law. This concept is also a fundamental part of American law. The IRS's own regulations, Section 1.501(c)(3)-1(d)(2), tells us what kind of activities tax-exempt organizations should be active in providing to society: "relief of the poor and distressed or of the underprivileged; . . . advancement of education; . . . *lessening the burdens of government;* and promotion of social welfare" (emphasis added).

These regulations read like they came directly out of Matthew, chapter 25. When the IRS tells us to take care of people in need, they are merely asking us to obey the Word of God.

Charitable and religious organizations are respected and blessed with tax exemption by the government because they benefit the public. Tax exemption is withheld or revoked when such organizations, in the view of the government, fail to provide these important public benefits.

Fortunately, revocation of tax-exempt status is still rare. However, the federal government and the IRS is indeed cracking down on all tax-exempt organizations.

Lessening the Burdens of Government

The Bible tells us to take care of widows, orphans, the sick, the poor, and the homeless. In general, the Word of God tells us to meet the social needs of people. These are legitimate commandments from God.

Our government also has an overriding interest in the welfare of its citizens. If we do not take care of these people in need, the government will. Because of the government's welfare burden, taxes are too high and likely to go higher still.

There is a direct and undeniable link between a failure to follow God's commandments and high taxes. Such a link is irrefutable. No one in government wants to pay the high price of social welfare: they provide social welfare only because they must. Government-provided welfare is expensive, and taxes are the only means by which we can pay the bill.

Lyndon Johnson's social program, called the Great American Dream, set the nation on the road to our current financial disaster by setting up a massive government-supported welfare structure. President Johnson made a second error in simultaneously trying to fight a very expensive war in Vietnam. Our nation could not do both without incurring massive federal deficits of $44.8 billion.[5]

Many of the programs in the Great American Dream are still with us today. Each year these programs cost more money as the needs and population expand. These programs were designed to help people in need: to feed the hungry, house the homeless, tend to the sick, educate the ignorant, and a variety of other noble goals. These programs have become an entrenched part of American political life, and people have come to depend upon the program. Without these programs, some people would literally starve.

Each president since has inherited these entrenched programs. No president has yet been able to reduce the escalating costs of these programs. At best some presidents claim to have slowed the growth in spending a little. There is little question that government spending is out of control. Social spending is the biggest reason our government is incurring debt beyond its income. Unfortunately, these programs seem to solve nothing.

Since 1963 when the government assumed responsibility for all of our social welfare, social problems have gone out of control: poverty, violence, promiscuous sexual activity, sexually transmitted diseases (AIDS!), suicides, teen suicides, the breakdown in education, violence, breakup of the family, high-school dropouts, etc.[6] Far more than liberal ideology is fueling this statistical nightmare. However, the liberal political ideology, embodied in the Great American Dream, is certainly a major contributing factor to the problem.

Our government cannot dispense social spending within the framework of Judeo-Christian morality and ethical constraints. To do so would clearly violate the law. However, to separate public welfare from godly morality, as our government must, is to court social chaos. Only in the private sector is it possible, and legal, to link welfare and morality.

Republicans and Democrats alike sincerely want government to be less expensive, taxes to be lower, and the public debt reduced. Both are trapped in a political tangle that may yet bankrupt the nation. High taxes will shut down the economy, and a dead economy can't pay taxes. With bills to pay and no taxes, we will have inflation, then hyper-inflation, followed by economic collapse. Through the looking glass of the Old Testament, this scenario is the judgment of God.

I do not believe this catastrophe is inevitable. We can heal our land and avoid this "Coming Economic Earthquake" as Mr. Larry Burkett calls it. I pray we can.

We Must Obey the Law

As Christians, we must submit to every ordinance of man for the Lord's sake, unless such an ordinance clearly violates the Word of God (1 Pet. 2:13-16). I have read the IRS's rules and regulations concerning tax-exempt organizations. As a Christian, I can tell you there is nothing in these rules or regulations that is a clear violation of the Word of God.

There is only one circumstance where a Christian is allowed to violate the laws of man—when that law clearly violates the Word of God. At that point, and only at that point, are we allowed an act of Christian civil disobedience. Christians have a long history of civil disobedience making martyrs of tens of thousands of godly people. Rarely has any legitimate act of civil disobedience ever involved taxation. Even John Bunyan, the famous English preacher who chose to spend thirteen years in a Bedford Jail, did not protest taxation. Pastor Bunyan's act of civil disobedience was in protest of England's licensing, accrediting, and approving of preachers. John Bunyan was violently opposed to a state-approved church.

Our Future: The State-approved Church

John Bunyan was right; we must not allow state accreditation of our religious organizations or our religious leaders. A state-controlled church has been the harshest judgment of God imposed upon the New Testament Church. It was the State Church that brought on the Dark Ages, "The Devil's millennium." It was the State Church that triggered the Inquisition. It was the State Church that started the fires in Northern Ireland that will not die out. It was the State Church that jailed John Bunyan, stood against Martin Luther, slaughtered the Scottish Covenateers and displayed their skulls in Edinburgh; indeed, it was the State Church that drove our forefathers from their homes to find freedom in America. A State-sponsored Church is an anathema to any true patriot and to any Christian believer.

A State Church cannot be created by political or social pressures, nor can it be prevented by passing laws. If America ever has to endure the indignity of a State Church, it will be because of the sins and negligence of Christian people (Matt. 25:41-46). Only Christian people can create or prevent a State Church.

The increased scrutiny of tax-exempt organizations by the federal government could lead us down the road of more federal control over religious organizations. A State Church can be created subtlety and accidently through neglect. Only four things are required to make a State Church:

1. State approval of religious organizations. This implies guidelines, rules, and regulations to be obeyed.[7]

2. The requirement that the State's policies be supported by religious organizations.[8]

3. The conviction by the State that it subsidizes these religious organizations.[9]

4. The desire to bend the Church away from God's will and make the Church conform to the will of the State as it becomes a tool of politics and policy rather than a servant of God.

We do not have a State-approved Church in America, yet! However, we could easily and accidently have a State Church soon. We do not currently have a State-controlled Church because the current guidelines given to the Church by the State do not clearly violate the Word of God. If current trends continue, these government guidelines could make the Church a servant to the State.

The modern political trend of politicians on both the Left and the Right to openly court the political participation of churches is dangerous in the extreme. Are they leading the Church into a politically polarized future? Are we already there? Is the next step to be a State-controlled Church? A State-controlled Church is not a road to freedom; it is a road to unmitigated disaster! We should avoid it at any cost. If the Church becomes polarized into competing political camps, we have already become a tool of the State and therefore rightly subject to State control.

Changes in our society and in our tax laws do seem to push religious organizations in an unpleasant and frightening direction of increased government control.

God Will Forgive Us

We can and must stop this legal drift towards increased control over the Church. However, the cause of this drift into statism must be clearly understood. Before we can protect our Church and heal our land we must deal with the root problem: sin in the Church. The sin of disobedience which crushed the Jewish nation is the same sin which threatens us and our freedom. Will God judge America any less harshly than He did His chosen people? I think not.

Isaiah 14:3 states, "And it shall come to pass in the day that the LORD shall give thee rest from thy sorrow, and from thy fear, and from the hard bondage wherein thou wast made to serve." God, even in judgment, is merciful and forgiving. Even now God will forgive us and heal our land. It is not too late.

Endnotes

1. B.B. Caldwell's sermon titled, "Seven World-Shaking Events Soon to Come to Pass."

2. *M'Culloch v. Maryland* (1819).

3. This is an example of what we in the tax business call "punitive taxation." Some of the penalty provision in our tax law are indeed punitive.

4. Worship of false gods was a problem in Israel: the false god Baal is mentioned fifty-one times in Scripture; Ashtaroth is mentioned eleven times; and Molech is mentioned eight times.

5. Every president since Mr. Lyndon Johnson, except for Mr. Clinton, has inherited the same error: massive social spending with massive military spending. No economy can support both. The end of the Cold War has allowed Mr. Clinton to reduce military spending somewhat, but not nearly enough to allow full funding of all the nation's social needs.

6. I refer you to an excellent little book, *America: To Pray or Not to Pray,* by David Barton (Aledo, TX: WallBuilder Press, 1991).

7. There are literally thousands of pages of law providing guidance to nonprofit organizations in the Internal Revenue Code, and the IRS's Rules and Regulations. Also, the IRS sincerely believes that they have the right to approve all tax-exempt organizations, even local churches.

8. The concept that a religious organization must conform to certain standards of public policy is a key idea of the Bob Jones case. *Bob Jones University v. U.S.,* 461 US 574 (1983), 103 S Ct 2017, 83-1 USTC P 9366, 52 AFTR2d 83-5001.

9. The idea that income tax exemption is, in and of itself, a direct subsidy is firmly fixed in tax law. In addition, many local governments believe they are unfairly forced to "subsidize" local churches by providing free police, fire, and other services to these tax-exempt organizations.

CHAPTER FOUR

Government Policy:
The Wrath of God

A Negative Trend

The disposition of our society toward nonprofit organizations, particularly the Church, has become increasingly more negative in the past thirty years.

An article entitled "Nonprofits under Scrutiny" appeared in the 16 June 1993 issue of the *Philadelphia Inquirer*. The article reports, in detail, a growing negative attitude in Congress and the IRS to nonprofit organizations. The first paragraph of this report said, "Members of Congress and the IRS agreed on the need to beef up penalties and add federal investigators to police the rapidly growing number of tax exempt groups."[1] Just what we all need, more tax penalties and more IRS agents!

The IRS has some deep concerns over the "lack of federal government control of nonprofit organizations under current law."[2] The IRS estimates that there are about 207,000 tax-exempt organizations that make no annual tax income filings with the IRS whatsoever. That's odd because all tax-exempt organizations must file an annual tax report with the IRS if revenues are over twenty-five thousand dollars.

The only exception to this rule requiring annual filings is for churches. Therefore, these 207,000 organizations that so deeply concern the IRS seem to be churches. Behind all the noble sounding discussion of nonfilers, lack of federal government oversight, etc., is that fact that the federal government believes it has the right to regulate these exempt organizations who currently do not file annual reports with the IRS. The only significant but legally nonfiling organizations are churches.

The IRS estimates that these nonfiling organizations have $674 billion in assets and annual tax-deductible contributions of at least $80 billion. Such IRS estimates are ridiculous—they are far too high. The numbers being tossed around by the IRS and Congress are designed to get your attention. They sure got mine! These estimates are also designed to justify the coming additional controls Congress may propose over nonfiling organizations such as churches.

One now former congressman, J.J. Pickle (D-Texas), made several cynical statements to which I took strong exception: "The tax exempt private sector is going to get bigger than the government," and, "Congress should impose a two year freeze on new applications for tax exempt status."[3] The most appalling quote in the *Philadelphia Inquirer* article is, "tax exemptions of nonprofit organizations *cost* the nation at least $36.5 billion a year in lost tax revenue." It seems that Congressman J.J. Pickle and the IRS agree that when a family gives money to their church it *costs* the federal government money.

Tax Expenditure Analysis, or Who Really Owns Your Money?

The current theory used by the federal government and the IRS to develop tax policy is called tax expenditure analysis.[4] The concept of federal tax expenditure analysis is based upon the idea that all the income of the nation belongs to the government. Tax rates below 100 percent, tax deductions, and nontaxable income (municipal bonds, housing allowances, etc.) are all tax expenditures that cost the nation revenues. The concept of tax expenditure analysis has been at the heart of federal tax policy for well over two decades. This theory of taxation underlies the modern attitude of the IRS and Congress concerning churches and other nonprofit organizations.

Language is important. It controls how a person thinks on any subject. The language of taxation directly affects the way Congress thinks about taxation. The language inherently a part of the tax expenditure analysis approach leads one to a socialistic view of the nation's wealth. It is this socialistic view that has allowed our nation's leaders to create a debt-spending crisis so gigantic that it may bankrupt the nation.

Tax Expenditure Analysis and Direct Public Subsidies

The 1983 Bob Jones doctrine effectively gave the tax expenditure analysis concept, as it applies to charitable organizations, the force of law. The Supreme Court ruled in *Bob Jones University v. U.S.* that nonprofit organizations, even nonprofit religious organizations, are subsidized by the federal government. Under the tax expenditure analysis theory, every nonprofit organization in America receives substantial support from the federal government that costs the nation at least $36.5 billion a year in lost tax revenue!

Tax Subsidies and the Death of the First Amendment

In the Bob Jones case, the Supreme Court effectively nullified the First Amendment's protection of religious nonprofit organizations by twisted application of this mythical tax subsidy. One of the key holdings in this landmark case is that religious organizations must conform to certain standards of "stated public policy," notwithstanding the fact that current standards of public policy may conflict with sincerely held convictions of faith, protected by the First Amendment. It is appalling to me that a mere pop-culture economic concept, such as tax expenditure analysis, is given enough legal weight to allow the Supreme Court to overturn such a crucial protection afforded by our Constitution.

The Bob Jones case is, in my opinion, one of the most important cases in the modern history of the Church. Interested Christians should be familiar with this far-reaching case. (see Appendix A.)

Declines in the Freedoms of Religion and Free Speech

The First Amendment protects two freedoms: freedom of speech and freedom of religion. Given how seriously the First Amendment's protections of religion have been weakened, it is logical that the next point of attack to occur would be an attack on religious free speech. The Bob Jones case was the most successful tax case in history to defeat the free exercise clause of the First Amendment. Bob Jones was followed by dozens of more recent cases that chip away at the remaining First Amendment protections.[5]

As expected, the next major attack on the First Amendment by the IRS would be an attempt to defeat one of the other freedoms protected by the First Amendment—free speech. In 1992, the IRS announced a major crackdown on the free speech of religious organizations.

The IRS Used As a Tool in Partisan Politics

When a political kingdom and God's kingdom clash, we have the potential for a serious crisis. To make matters worse, when the IRS enforces these new legal restrictions on free speech, they tend to do so in a partisan political manner. One of many ironies of the Bob Jones case is this: the new law's stated purpose was to fight discrimination, yet the partisan political manner in which the Bob Jones doctrine is applied creates discrimination, political discrimination. The federal government is guilty of the crime they alleged against Bob Jones.

In January 1992, the IRS revealed a strategy to defeat religious free speech. The IRS publicized a statement from Jimmy Swaggart Ministries (JSM) in which it agreed to IRS findings that it had supported Pat Robertson for president in 1988 and thereby engaged in campaign activities prohibited by Internal Revenue Code Section 501. The facts were clear: Jimmy Swaggart voiced his support for candidate Robertson from the pulpit at official functions of the ministry, and Swaggart encouraged the members of Jimmy Swaggart Ministries to work for and vote for candidate Robertson. Also, in *The Evangelist* newsletter, Jimmy Swaggart Ministries issued an endorsement of Pat Robertson's candidacy for president. Clearly, Jimmy Swaggart Ministries violated the campaign provision of Internal Revenue Code Section 501. Even with this violation, the IRS did not revoke the 501(c)(3) status of Jimmy Swaggart Ministries; a public apology and a promise to do better next time were the full extent of IRS "punishment" for this errant ministry.

Internal Revenue Code Section 501(c)(3) is the law which grants churches and other nonprofit organizations coveted tax-exempt status. This status allows churches to receive tax-deductible contributions from individuals and to avoid paying income taxes on the receipt of these donations. To aid understanding of this discussion, I will cite a small portion of the last sentence of Code Section 501(c)(3) concerning an organization: "[An organization] which does not participate in, or intervene in (including the publishing or distributing of statements), any political campaign on behalf of (or in opposition to) any candidate for public office." This sentence clearly makes it illegal for any organization described in Section 501(c)(3) to engage in political campaign activities. This flat prohibition is much more complex than a mere statement.

Where Did This Crazy Tax Law Come From?

The last sentence to Internal Revenue Code Section 501(c)(3) was made as a floor amendment by freshman Sen. Lyndon Johnson of Texas in 1954. Mr. Johnson's campaign to the United States Senate was opposed by a conservative religious organization, but Mr. Lyndon Johnson became senator in spite of this opposition. The floor amendment to Section 501(c)(3) was payback for this opposition. The amendment was unanimously passed without debate.

Making floor amendments is a poor way to create new tax law. It circumvents the normal due process of law, depriving the public of their opportunity to lobby Congress. The lack of public hearings, committee reports, and input from the Internal Revenue Service and the Department of Justice, or even the staff lawyers assigned to Congress, means that very bad law is often passed as floor amendments. This amendment of Section 501(c)(3) is bad law, so bad that for forty years the IRS would not even enforce the law!

Why Did the IRS Refuse to Enforce the Law?

The IRS does not tell me why they do things. Until 1992 the IRS had only attempted to enforce the law one time in court.[6] It is my belief that the IRS wisely refused to enforce this new law for a variety of reasons.

• The IRS avoids hotly contested constitutional debates. Significant constitutional issues are raised by this strange floor amendment.

• IRS field agents are not trained to study free speech. Like most accountants, IRS agents are trained to investigate financial transactions. IRS auditors deal with numbers. Yet, in this law, Congress gave them orders to evaluate the content of free speech.

• The IRS is very careful to avoid the appearance that they are a tool of partisan political interest. The IRS will try their best to avoid being used in this political fashion. However, any attempt to evaluate the content of free speech is going to make the IRS a tool of partisan political interest; it is unavoidable.

Why Enforce the Law Now?

In January 1992, almost forty years after it was passed, the IRS announced it would begin to enforce the law. Something does not smell right! Why does the IRS find it must now enforce the law?

The root of this newfound concern is the rise of the Christian Right as a powerful political movement. Liberal congressional concern is specifically targeted at the Christian Right. This movement challenged entrenched political interest in our country. Liberal congressmen and senators object to political challenges that may cost them their jobs. These congressional concerns are by their nature partisan. Neither Congress nor the IRS can avoid the charge that the IRS is being politically manipulated.

Politically Active Churches Have Blessed America

The political history of churches and religious organizations in our nation is well documented. Our nation is much better today because of the political activities of churches. One of the most obvious examples is the civil rights movement—a very unpopular movement in its day. Now most Americans look back on the black Church's accomplishments in the 1950s and 1960s with pride. Not pride as black folks or white folks, but as Americans. Enforcement of this 1954 law would have hindered this important social movement. The IRS wisely stayed out of the civil rights debate.

The black Church has a proud history of political activism. Today, the black Church is still active. In the 1992 presidential race, President Clinton spoke in a prominent black church in Detroit. The church even passed the collection plate for political contributions. This *is* a political use of a church, but it is not wrong.

The National Baptist Convention met in New York City in the summer of 1993. In newspapers and news reports on radio and television, the National Baptist Convention endorsed a black man running for a second term as mayor of New York. A public endorsement! Precisely the facts in the Jimmy Swaggart case. Please allow me to make a prediction: the National Baptist Convention will not be challenged by the IRS on this issue. They will not be forced to issue a public settlement agreement as was Jimmy Swaggart Ministries. And, the National Baptist Convention will continue to exercise their rights to endorse, support, and campaign for candidates for political office, as they should.

Politically Active Churches Are Not Wrong

This endorsement by the National Baptist Convention is a clear violation of Section 501 (c)(3) of the tax law, but it is not wrong. The National Baptist Convention has a right to endorse candidates for public office. This right is fixed by their traditions and political history, a history from which all Americans have benefited. The IRS will not challenge the National Baptist Convention. Any attempt to do so will embarrass the IRS and Congress.

Enforcement action by the IRS of this stupid 1954 law is partisan politics at its worst. The IRS vigorously attacks the Christian Right yet avoids any controversy of the more traditional Christian centers of political power such as the National Baptist Convention.

Victims of the IRS's Partisan Political Activity

Jerry Falwell

In 1994, Jerry Falwell's Old Time Gospel Hour agreed to pay fifty thousand dollars of taxes for "improper political activities" which occurred in 1986 and 1987. The IRS investigated Dr. Falwell's ministry for four years. Dr. Falwell agreed to pay the tax only as a condition for having his tax-exempt status reinstated, not because he believed his ministry did anything wrong.

A big issue the IRS found was that Old Time Gospel Hour employees, on their own time, were active in conservative political campaigns. The IRS was a little excessive in their efforts to shutdown the Old Time Gospel Hour's access to the political process. Uncharacteristically, Dr. Falwell folded due to financial pressure.

Dr. Falwell's outspoken political activities and social commentaries have cost him a huge amount of money. Dirty tricks, like flooding his telephone lines and publicly disputing the revocation of his tax-exempt status, have seriously damaged the finances of Dr. Falwell's ministry.

As of 5 April 1993, The Old Time Gospel Hour had debts of $37.6 million and $73 million at Liberty Bible College. The Associated Press, on 31 October 1993, reported that Liberty Bible College narrowly avoided a second foreclosure attempt.

Pat Robertson

Pat Robertson's Christian Coalition is different from a 501(c)(3); it is a 501(c)(4) organization. Pat Robertson and the Christian Coalition seem to have some allegation or lawsuit filed against it almost daily. Although these allegations and lawsuits imply wrongdoing, a 501(c)(4) organization is allowed to participate in political activities. The same folks who want to remove Dr. Falwell as a center of political influence in America also want to eliminate Pat Robertson's influence.

Please allow me to make another prediction: Pat Robertson will be at the center of a firestorm of political and legal attacks. These future attacks will involve the IRS, class action lawsuits, maybe even allegations of criminal misconduct. Do I believe Pat is guilty of any misconduct? No! In my opinion, Pat Robertson is above reproach, but I do know that many powerful political groups are near terrified of his substantial influence.

These frightened people will do anything in an effort to undermine Pat's influence: making false accusations and charges, filing frivolous lawsuits, flooding his telephone lines to cut off financial support, and other dishonest actions. In my opinion, none of these ministries did anything wrong.

The IRS's Power to Revoke Tax Exemption

The IRS has the power to retroactively revoke an organization's tax-exempt status.[7] Before it issues a revocation, the IRS must determine for itself that:

1. An important fact or misstatement was made in the original application for exempt status.

2. The operations are different from the original representations in the application for exempt status.

3. The organization has engaged in a prohibited transaction. Political activities are, in the IRS view, prohibited.

Tax-exempt organizations are not protected against retroactive revocations.[8] Such organizations have the right to appeal IRS revocation by going directly to the IRS appeals office. One appeals an IRS decision by protesting directly to the IRS! Not only do we have the IRS as judge and jury but as the court of appeals as well.

The problems with this process are obvious. However, there is a less obvious problem. The appeals process inside the IRS takes time. The last time I suggested to an IRS tax-exempt field examiner that I planned to appeal his determination to revoke an organization's tax exemption, he told me to count on a two-year delay before I could get an appointment. Apparently, there is a huge backlog of cases. Two years! I wonder how many politically motivated revocations are already in the pipeline.

How long can a tax-exempt organization financially survive an initial revocation? Can they continue to receive contributions in good conscience? What is the impact upon a ministry operating under a cloud, a cloud so serious it could threaten the very existence of a ministry?

An organization under IRS threat of revocation cannot go to the courts seeking an injunction to stop the IRS.[9] Only after an organization has been revoked can it appeal to the courts for a judicial determination. Once again we have the same problem: how long can an organization financially survive revocation of their exempt status? Judicial determination can take three to five years. During this time, the IRS publicly identifies the ministry as one "no longer able to receive tax deductible contributions." This IRS power to revoke is awesome. It is the power to financially destroy a ministry!

Jerry Falwell's Revocation

Other than what I read in the paper, I know very little of the details which led to the revocation of Jerry Falwell's ministry, the

Old Time Gospel Hour. I know that employees of the Old Time Gospel Hour, on their own initiative and on their own time, were active in political campaigns. They used copy machines, paper clips, and other incidental supplies purchased by the Old Time Gospel Hour and may also have used the telephones to a limited degree.

On this basis the IRS revoked the tax-exempt status of the Old Time Gospel Hour. The amount of direct money spent on political campaign activities by this ministry was zero. The indirect money spent was insignificant. However, the language of the law prohibiting political campaign activities is absolute, i.e., you can spend nothing whatsoever on political campaign activities.

I believe that the Old Time Gospel Hour would have won a case in court protesting this revocation. However, after a three-to-five year court battle, contributions would have dried up; the Old Time Gospel Hour would not exist.

The IRS has signaled its willingness to rely on the threat of revocation in their efforts to police religious organizations. They used the threat to bend Jimmy Swaggart; they actually revoked Jerry, later reinstated him, and have systematically threatened my smaller ministry clients with revocation.

A Nationwide Crisis

I directly know of other ministries of superb quality whose financial existence is being threatened by the same forces attempting to destroy these national ministries. I am compelled not to name names for fear of causing more damage to these important members of the kingdom of God. When a ministry has an IRS problem, a lawsuit, or a financial crisis, do not participate in the work of the enemy by thinking to yourself, what did they do wrong? These threatened ministries may have done nothing wrong. If fact, it may be what they have done *right* that is the root of their troubles.

Moderate Ministries

There has been no public mention of a single liberal or moderate ministry being challenged by the IRS for their political activities. I have already mentioned the National Baptist Convention and their very public endorsement of a candidate for mayor of

New York City. Consider also the Rainbow Coalition voter registration drives which "refused" to allow Republicans to register; First Baptist Church in Detroit which will conduct political fundraising during church services; the Southern Christian Leadership Conference which routinely supports political candidates and social legislation. Are these fine ministries doing anything wrong? Should the IRS go after them too? Of course not. They are perfectly within their constitutional rights. I have no complaints against these ministries. In fact, I admire them and their intended good for America.

The issue is not what these ministries are doing. The issue is why are conservative ministries being attacked for doing exactly the same thing more moderate (liberal) ministries are doing and have been doing for many years. The point is that IRS enforcement of this restriction on political activities is, by definition, partisan politics at its very worst. Any enforcement of a law restricting free speech is unconstitutional.[10]

The New Jersey Election Fiasco

Christine Todd Whitman, a conservative Republican, scored an upset victory over incumbent Gov. Jim Florio, a traditional tax and spend liberal. Before Mrs. Whitman could even assume the office of governor of New Jersey the liberals cried, foul! It seems that Mr. Ed Rollins, the GOP campaign manager, in a fit of braggadocios euphoria, "Spun Himself Out of Control."[11] If he lied, he told a whopper! Mr. Rollins said he distributed "$500,000 in walking around" money to keep black churches out of the campaign. Black pastors were encouraged not to campaign for Governor Florio. He later said he lied. This event was total fiction.

There are two important points to this 1993 headline news that the media has overlooked: first, a conservative Republican, Christine Whitman, received over 25 percent of votes that were cast by blacks; and second, for a black pastor and black church to be involved in a political campaign to any extent whatsoever is, according to the IRS, against the law. Even if Ed Rollins did what he initially said he did, he was merely paying people to obey the law.

Over 25 Percent of Blacks Voted for a Conservative

Black people are not blind sheep to be manipulated by their so-called leaders. "Walking around" money will not change the way our black citizens vote to any significant degree. A conservative Republican is not going to get 25 percent of the black vote merely on someone's say-so! Many blacks are beginning to recognize the false promises of the post-1963 liberals, many have conservative Christian roots to which they are returning.

Most blacks of a generation ago have conservative family values that now look very attractive in light of society's decline, and most now realize they have gained very little ground socially or economically following after the false teachers of liberalism in America.

I predict that the trickle of blacks into the conservative political ranks will become a flood. It will be slow at first. They have been told that conservatives are all racist for so long, many believe this lie too. But, the truth will come out and finally set God's people free.

Black Churches Can't Campaign

Black pastors and black churches, according to the IRS, cannot be involved in a political campaign to any extent whatsoever. It is against the law! As to the involvement (or lack thereof) in the New Jersey election scandal, since when is paying people to obey the law a crime? Liberals want to have it both ways. They actively put pressure on the IRS to suppress the conservative Christian political movement and freak-out with any suggestion that the liberal or moderate Christian political movement is being suppressed. In the best possible light, this sounds like partisan politics to me. At its very worst, it looks like racial politics, something we should have left behind in the 1950s.

What Could Be Worse?

According to the Montgomery, Alabama, *Advertiser*,

> Ed Rollins said he paid black ministers in New Jersey $500,000 not to mention voting to their constituents on the Sunday before the election. Richard Shelby provided money for black ministers in Birmingham to work their

constituents so they could be given marked ballots and herded to the polls like sheep. Who is the most evil?[12]

Good question!

I can tell you what is worse. Our own government using every means available to stifle free political speech for some and encourage it for others, that is worse. All in government service are sworn to protect the Constitution, not distort its meaning. To stifle anyone's free political speech is a serious distortion of our guaranteed liberties.

In effect, we either have free political speech for everyone or speech is an endangered liberty. The IRS is our government's chief policeman designated to shutdown the political activities of nonprofit ministries. It is a fact, the IRS is policing the free speech of conservative Christian organizations.

The Impact on the IRS

Every year it seems as if the public's respect for the IRS drops another notch or two. American taxpayers do not trust the IRS. I do not believe the IRS's public image can survive the kind of massive political crisis that attacks on free speech will trigger. The IRS is very sensitive to any charge of being a partisan political tool. Such a charge, if it were to stick, would seriously damage their effectiveness. The IRS has been politically manipulated in the past, most notably under President Nixon. More recently, Bob Dole asked the IRS to shutdown the Unification Church and put the Reverend Sun Moon in jail.[13]

Sen. Bob Dole sent a letter of complaint concerning Mr. Sun Myung Moon, dated 9 January 1976, to the commissioner of the Internal Revenue Service. In the letter, Mr. Dole gave as one reason to attack Rev. Sun Moon: "Mr. Moon has made several statements implying political and governmental objectives." I find it ironic that a so-called conservative would be one of the first to politically manipulate the IRS in an attack on religion. What Senator Dole did was wrong.

There is now intense pressure on the IRS by liberal members of Congress to shutup conservative ministries. Just like Bob Dole, they write letters to the commissioner of the Internal Revenue Service asking the IRS to investigate a ministry. To these official letters are attached alleged political statements made in newsletters or in public statements. The IRS is under intense pressure to crackdown on political activities of tax-exempt organizations. To the IRS, the First Amendment is not even an issue. The issue is Section 501 of the Internal Revenue Code.

It's Not Fair!

No one has ever said to me that tax law is fair. It is not fair—it was never intended to be fair. Tax law is designed to accomplish only two purposes for Congress: raise federal revenues and achieve the social-economic agenda of Congress.[14] There is little logic in tax law, and there is no concept of equity in tax law. Tax law is exclusively a matter of statutory language in the Internal Revenue Code.

The current position of the IRS and Congress is clear: no tax-exempt organization can be politically active. Political activities cost money. According to the tax expenditure analysis theory, that money all came from the federal government to the nonprofit organizations as an act of grace. The position of the IRS and Congress is that such organizations cannot use federal money to influence public policy. According to the IRS, Congress, and the Supreme Court, this is not a violation of the Constitution's protection of free speech. Howard M. Schoenfeld, a top IRS official, explains, "You can have all the politically oriented free speech you want so long as you do not use tax subsidized money to pay for the privilege."

Because of the tax expenditure theory, Congress and the IRS believe they have the right to directly intervene into the free speech of nonprofit organizations if such speech has political overtones. Apparently, many in the IRS believe that such intervention can be done in a partisan political manner. It is a fact that IRS political intervention occurs in a partisan manner. One can only conclude that such intervention is partisan by design. This situation is becoming a matter of liberty!

The use of taxation and the application of tax expenditure analysis theory in an effort to control churches and other nonprofit organizations is our society's harsh judgment upon us as an ineffective Church.

The First Amendment was designed to protect three basic freedoms: the freedom of speech and the two freedoms of religion. The purpose of the First Amendment was to insure that a free press and a free religious community could watch-dog the federal government as the legendary forth-estate of government.

Without Free Speech, How Can We Correct Ourselves?

The forth-estate has a variety of functions: to protect the rights of the governed, expose abuses of power, to provide positive leadership on matters of morality, and to insure the public's input into the government's policy debates. The free speech to be protected by the First Amendment was both political and religious speech, but now our government is moving to restrict free speech in the context of religious and charitable organizations.[15] By definition, this is a constitutional crisis which weakens America in a fundamental way. Without free speech, our nation will lose the ability to self-correct errors that creep into society.

The Rise of the State-approved Church

These freedoms of religion guaranteed that government would never establish an official religion and that religion would be free from the government's interference. This was to prevent any law endorsing or establishing an official government-approved State Church. The Constitution guarantees that the government could not force us to be all Catholic, Anglican, Baptist, or any other denomination.

Our Founding Fathers never envisioned the First Amendment's freedoms of religion as restricting religious activity or expression in our society by citizens! Until 1963, the establishment clause was always presumed to be a restriction on government-sponsored denominational activities. In 1963, the meaning of the establishment clause of the First Amendment was changed, so it is now a restriction on expressions of religion or religious activities by citizens. If we have twisted the Constitution so it now stands on its head, have we protected freedom or undermined it? Have we already become an Orwellian society where yes means no and no means yes?

These religious rights were political rights as well as theological. The basic outline of the Constitution is that all rights belong to the people or to the states unless specifically granted to the federal government in the Constitution. The power to police religion is clearly granted to no one and must therefore remain with the people.

Our freedoms in this nation come from our most basic political concept: government by the consent of the governed. The greatest fear of our Founding Fathers was that the federal government would grow too powerful and too large. Every tiny bit of power that is accumulated by the federal government can only come from one source: the rights of the people who are governed. Every time the federal government gains more power, the people have less power. Every dollar the federal government takes in taxation is an economic vote denied the people. Freedom and the economy are clearly related.

A Modern Prophet

Many years ago, I was privileged to hear Dr. Joseph Lowery, chairman of the Southern Christian Leadership Conference, say, "None of us are free unless all of us are free." This truth has stayed with me and became part of my personal philosophy. Freedom for only one group of people is not freedom; at best, it is the illusion of freedom. When one freedom is attacked or weakened, it is inevitable that other freedoms will begin to fall, like dominos.

America must always be in the process of becoming free. If not, the dream that is the hope of America will fade. The first and most important function of government is to protect the freedoms of its citizens. When a government uses its power to limit or restrict basic freedoms, it can become the worst broker of slavery, enslaving the very people it means to protect. When the power of government is used to limit freedom, the government must ultimately become corrupt. There can be nothing more corrupt than a slave merchant.

It is essential to the future of the American Dream that the power of government be committed to maximizing individual liberty, never to limiting the freedom of the people. The American Dream is still just that, a dream, a bright hope, but merely a hope. We must not allow hope to die. This is a fundamental mission shared by the Church and our nation: hope.

Endnotes

1. Gilbert M. Gauland and Neill A. Borowski, "Nonprofits under Scrutiny," *Philadelphia Inquirer*, 16 June 1993, 1.

2. On 9 July 1993, Howard M. Schoenfeld, a top IRS official in the area of tax-exempt organizations, made a speech to the Non-for-Profit Industry Conference sponsored by the American Institute of Certified Public Accountants.

3. Personally, I do not see anything wrong with the private sector being bigger than the government. In my opinion, having a government bigger than the private sector is both wrong and stupid.

4. The tax expenditure analysis concept has been around in one form or another in our nation for about thirty years. The current popular version was developed in 1978 by the Brookings Institution.

5. Faith Baptist School in Louisville, Nebraska, where a pastor and seven deacons were jailed. Also see *Reagan v. Taxation with Representation of Washington*, Grove City College and cases following these lines.

6. This is a special case. Christian Echoes lied to the IRS on their application for tax-exempt status. In court, memorandums describing how they planned to deceive the IRS proved compelling. Even with this dishonest behavior, there are many important flaws in this case that give it little precedent-setting value.

7. It is a well-established principle of tax law that the taxpayer is guilty until he is proven innocent. The revocation of tax-exempt status demonstrates this concept of law well. The IRS must determine as judge, jury, and executioner.

8. Rev. Proc 93-4, S 12.08, 1993-1 IRB 83.

9. This principle was established in *Bob Jones University v. Simon*. Odd how Bob Jones keeps popping up in our discussions of IRS power over tax-exempt organizations.

10. See Edward McGlynn Gaffner, Jr., "On Not Rendering to Caesar: The Unconstitutionality of Tax Regulation of Activities of Religious Organizations Related to Politics," *De Paul Law Review* (Fall 1990): 1–52.

11. *Washington Post*, 21 November 1993.

12. Montgomery, Alabama, *Advertiser*, 29 November 1993.

13. I am not friend of Rev. Sun Moon. I believe he and the Unification Church are a dangerous religious cult. However, the First Amendment protects everybody or it protects nobody. As Christians, we have effective ways to deal with cults: prayer, the Word of God, education, and effective ministry.

14. Federal tax policy is written to do more than merely raise revenues. Tax policy is also written to encourage or discourage certain activities. For example, if Congress wants to encourage building of low income housing for the poor, a tax law giving developers a "tax break" will encourage such social policy. The tax law is as much about social policy as it is about financing the business of government.

15. I find it odd that at the same time our government is moving to restrict political and religious free speech, it seems to be protecting pornography, representations of violence, and other forms of vulgarity in the name of free speech.

CHAPTER FIVE

Our Duty:
Christian Ethics and Tax Law

Tax Protestors

Frustration with the IRS and Congress will eventually lead to a ballot-box revolution. That's good. Our Founding Fathers envisioned such revolutions. Thomas Jefferson believed the new nation needed a revolution about every twenty years. I agree; what America needs is a peaceful, legal, and political revolution that will put us back on the road of maximum freedom for all Americans. Freedom for the few is no freedom at all; at best, it is the illusion of freedom. My prayer is, "Lord, make all your children free!"

Unfortunately, I already see elements of the coming revolution that are not legal nor acceptable in any moral sense. The growing tax protestor movement is the vanguard of revolution. This movement is illegal, unfortunate, and also unnecessary. It is merely people responding to their fears and frustrations in the only way they know how.

I have seen some tax protestor literature, and it makes me furious. In many cases they have the gall to link the word *patriot* with their illegal and unpatriotic ideas. *Patriot* is a holy word; a tax protestor is just a criminal. Some of these criminals are Christians. Unfortunately, the terms *Christian* and *criminal* are not mutually exclusive.

We have a dear lady who infrequently drops by our office for free tax advice. She is a totally beautiful eighty-plus-year-old lady, about ninety pounds of pure spunk and a deeply committed Christian. She is also a tax protestor.

She comes to see me because she is so terrified of the IRS. She gets upset and cries; soon all the ladies in the office are crying. It really is a mess. The problem is that this dear lady refuses to file her tax returns. I always give her the same advice: I can't help you unless you file your tax returns. She is adamant; she will not file because she is ashamed of her government. She believes the federal government uses her tax money to kill millions of babies each year.

The problem is that this dear lady has listened to false teachings on Christian obligations to taxing authorities. The results are devastating. The IRS has seized her bank accounts, levied fines and penalties against her that far exceed her taxes. This lady has made a serious mistake.

There is great danger in following zealots who teach against taxation as ungodly. Acts 5:37 reminds us, "After this man rose up Judas of Galilee in the days of the taxing, and drew away much people after him: he also perished; and all, [even] as many as obeyed him, were dispersed."

A Church As a Tax Protestor

False teachings can invade a whole Christian movement. Such teachings do not make the movement un-Christian, but it certainly will lead Christians into sin. When Christians live in sin, the results are always devastating.

There are large groups of churches in the Apostolic tradition that have pastors who pay little, if any, taxes. Churches in the Apostolic tradition generally have two offerings in a worship service. The first, called the tithe, according to their traditions, is holy and set aside for the ministers. The second is called an offering and is for the needs of the congregation such as building maintenance and teaching materials. Apostolic churches trace these practices to certain Old Testament religious statutes to support the physical and financial needs of the Hebrew priest and temple.

These traditions are beautiful and holy and based upon the long-standing traditions of their faith. These traditions are not wrong. What's wrong is that some pastors treat this as a love gift and do not pay taxes on the income.[1] In the past, such a failure to pay taxes was due to ignorance of the tax law. Now, a failure to pay taxes is due to a stubborn and misguided notion that they shouldn't have to pay taxes on the money because of their religious traditions.

Several years ago, the IRS helped clear up misconceptions about taxation of ministers in the Apostolic tradition. One minister in the Apostolic tradition was audited by the IRS. He protested to the IRS agent who was doing his audit saying, "No minister in my denomination pays taxes on his *Tithe* income." As a result of this minister's objection, the IRS audited every minister in a small Apostolic denomination in the Ohio Valley. None of the ministers had ever paid taxes on the tithe income they had received. The IRS examiners got each and every one of them!

In recent years, education of ministers has corrected many tax misconceptions. There are still stubborn people, however, who refuse to comply with the tax law.

An Honest Tax Protester

Many people think they are tax protesters when they are not. If a taxpayer has a moral conviction that some specific tax law is wrong, he has a right to become a conscientious objector, i.e., a tax protestor. The best definition I have ever heard defining conviction is a moral belief for which you are willing to die.[2] In my opinion, there is very little in tax law for which I am willing to die, but I cannot make moral judgments on behalf of other Christians.

An honest tax protester must be willing to bear the full legal responsibility for any act of civil disobedience. These consequences include public embarrassment, fines, and prison. Most important of all, an honest tax protester cannot hide from the IRS. The IRS must be notified that you are a tax protestor. I suggest the easiest way to notify the IRS of your moral convictions is to file the required IRS Form 1040. Each page of which must be clearly marked, "This return is filed under protest" in bright red ink. The exact nature of your protest should be spelled out in detail on the face of the return or in an attached memorandum. You will have the satisfaction of knowing that you are an honest tax protestor. Sit back and wait for the IRS to come get you; they will.

A person who does not file a tax return is not a tax protestor; he is a tax cheat! A protest, by definition, cannot occur in secret.

A secret protest is no protest whatsoever. It reminds me of a secret Christian.

Please be honest in your tax dealings. If you believe you must be a tax protestor, be an honest protestor! I know of very few honest tax protestors. Any fool can be a tax cheat; it requires no morals or convictions whatsoever. A nonfiler is a tax cheat.

The Example of Christ

Jesus gave us valid examples of how we should deal with taxation and the IRS. Jesus had at least two personal friends who were tax collectors, the IRS agents of their day (see Luke 5:27 and Luke 19:2–5), and Scripture implies Jesus had many tax collectors as friends.[3] Jesus consistently refused to judge tax collectors.

When Jesus gave advice on taxation, he was directly on point: "Render unto Caesar the things which are Caesar's and unto God the things which are God's" (Matt. 22:21).

The lesson is clear. It is not my lesson; it is direct from our Lord: as Christians we have an obligation to fully obey the tax law. We can and should actively work to change bad tax law, but even as we work to change bad tax laws we must obey the law.

I have no tolerance with so-called Christian tax protesters. The phrase itself, "Christian tax protesters," is to me a contradiction of terms. It distresses me that such tax protest movements abound. I read all the tax protestor cases that run across my desk. Many tax protests have a religious element. Not only does a tax protest lack sound Christian doctrine, it is stupid!

The Criminal Investigation Division of the IRS, the same division that put Al Capone away, deals with tax protestors. They have incredible resources to capture and deal with tax protestors. The proliferation of computer power in our economy and inside the IRS will make nonfilers and other tax protestors more easily captured.

The IRS invests significantly more money into finding tax protestors than the tax revenues their capture will create. The IRS invests so heavily into finding and punishing tax protestors because they believe tax protestors undermine the integrity of the entire tax system. The punishment is severe and often public. As a minimum, a tax protestor will pay at least twice the taxes he would have paid if his return was filed honestly. Tax protestors often have fines levied against them by federal judges. These fines can be as low as ten thousand dollars, but fines in the one hundred thousand dollars to five hundred thousand dollars range are not uncommon. In some cases called jeopardy assessments, fines can be in the multiple millions of dollars. Jail terms are common in tax protestor cases. An eighteen month sentence is routinely applied to even modest tax protestors. Al Capone spent most of the rest of his life in jail and was released only as an invalid to die at home.

Is the Church a Sovereign Power in Matters of Taxation?

According to our doctrines of faith, and according to our nation's Constitution, churches and religious organizations are exempt from all forms of taxation including, I might add, social security taxes, which churches have been required to pay since 1984. However, Jesus, who is Lord over the Church, submitted himself to unfair taxation as an example to us (see Matt. 17:24–27). To refuse to comply with the tax law is to deny Christ! But, is the Church a sovereign power in matters of taxation? No!

Christ Is King

The Church is not sovereign; she is a servant, literally a slave of Jesus Christ, our King (Rom. 14:11). The disciples had a lot of trouble understanding the nature of Jesus' kingdom. When James and John were lobbying for prime ministerships, they were really thinking in political terms, not spiritual (see Matt. 20:21).

Jesus made it very plain that His kingdom is not of this world (John 18:36). Jesus pointedly denied every opportunity to claim any civil authority whatsoever. He is head of the Church and our Lord. For the Church to claim civil authority in light of His example would be inappropriate. To grant the Church civil authority would clearly set us on the road to a State Church. A path we, as Christians, dare not tread.

Jesus also taught us by example. The only place in Scripture where Jesus worked a miracle with even a hint of personal benefit was a miracle to pay His taxes. The tax collectors asked Peter if his Master was going to pay taxes. Without consulting Jesus, Peter quickly answered yes. (Peter was always a little nervous before authority until a resurrected Jesus met him on the beach to talk about it. Even after that, Peter often had trouble dealing with authority.)

Jesus made it clear that He was exempt from taxes. (How can Caesar be over God or tax God?) Yet, Jesus agreed to submit to man's taxation as a lesson to us that we should always pay our taxes, "lest we should offend them" (Matt. 17:24–27).

Should the Church Be Tax Exempt As Was Our Lord?

Tax exemption is a privilege to be granted and is based upon a positive performance and influence in society. It is not a right to be demanded. Tax exemption must be earned by our actions in the kingdoms of this world. The Church should be tax exempt; however, such a token of respect from our society must be earned.

The Bible lays out clearly the ministries we are to be active in the kingdoms of this world: care for the widowed and orphaned, feed and clothe the poor, house the homeless, tend the sick, the prisoners, etc. It is by our own biblical standards that we are to be judged. At this point in history, our society has judged us to be less than worthy.

Is It Right to Pay Taxes for Evil Uses?

This is the most difficult question in any discussion of Christian ethics and tax law. It would be a mistake to rely upon our own wisdom when we have the Bible to teach us by example.

The dear lady we discussed at the beginning of this chapter is deeply and morally offended by abortion. She refuses to pay her taxes because she believes the federal government is literally killing millions of babies. She may have her facts right; however, her conclusions are wrong.

Mary and Joseph, the earthly parents of Jesus, voluntarily paid their taxes to a government known for its brutality:

> And it came to pass in those days, that there went out a decree from Caesar Augustus that all the world should be taxed. (And this taxing was first made when Cyrenius was governor of Syria.) And all went to be taxed, every one into his own city. And Joseph also went up from Galilee, out of the city of Nazareth, into Judaea, . . . to be taxed with Mary his espoused wife, being great with child. (Luke 2:1–5)

These taxes were paid to a government that killed babies: "Then Herod, when he saw that he was mocked of the wise men, was exceeding wrath, and sent forth, and slew all the children that were in Bethlehem, and in all the coasts thereof, from two years old and under, according to the time which he had diligently inquired of the wise men" (Matt. 2:16).

Jesus paid His taxes and taught His followers to pay their taxes. Jesus' teachings on taxation are rich and poignant. These taxes were to be paid to a government that murdered John the Baptist. Jesus often predicted His own murder at the hands of this same government. I sometimes wonder if the coin found in the fish's mouth purchased the spikes that nailed him to that tree. Even if Jesus knew that to be true, He would have paid His taxes anyway. Jesus instructed us to pay taxes to a government He knew to be corrupt. And, Peter reinforced Jesus' teachings on obedience to governmental authorities: "Submit yourselves to every ordinance of man for the Lord's sake" (1 Pet. 2:13). Furthermore, Paul reinforced Jesus' teachings on obedience to governmental authorities: "Render therefore to all their dues: tribute to whom tribute is due; custom to whom custom; fear to whom fear; honor to whom honor" (Rom. 13:7).

The reason Congress and the IRS are cracking down on ministries may be that they sense an unbiblical and unlawful attitude among some Christians in matters of taxation. With teachings this powerful, what options do we have as Christians other than to pay our taxes as Jesus paid His. The IRS may well be a dangerous tool, like Assyria or Babylon, to teach God's people how to live obediently.

Case Study: The Abusive IRS Agent

In my career, I have only met one abusive IRS agent, and he retired over ten years ago. This guy was legendary for losing his temper and yelling at taxpayers and CPAs. When I first met this agent, I did not know of his reputation.

As a young CPA, I had the bad luck of having a hot-tempered IRS agent for my first office audit. He got upset with me for answering questions directed to the taxpayer. With a power of attorney, I have a perfect right to answer these questions. He jumped up yelling at me to the top of his lungs. I was stunned. Although I rarely lose my temper, I jumped up and yelled back at him. I told him to get his supervisor out here immediately. We were going to discuss his conduct with his supervisor. Believe me, this agent's supervisor made sure that I did not have to deal with another fit of his ill temper. This IRS will not tolerate unprofessional conduct by their employees.

Our temper problem was resolved and our IRS audit was quickly completed with no additional taxes due. The point of this case study is that IRS management does not condone abusive behavior by IRS employees on any level. If you suggest to IRS management that an agent is being abusive, I know for a fact that management will look into the matter.

Case Study: The Christian Blacksmith

I love talking about business. When I meet a new friend there are two things I immediately want to talk about: Jesus and business—in that order. Recently, I met a Christian blacksmith. Once matters of faith were established, I talked to him about his business.

This young, fifty-year-old blacksmith was, as he called it, "semi-retired." He had a beautiful big truck and trailer, fully equipped for the blacksmith trade He called it a "rig."

It seems he had a thriving family-owned company in the ornamental iron work business. He made a good living: forty-five thousand dollars and, in a good year, fifty thousand dollars. He said he tried to run his business as a Christian until he had his first encounter with an IRS audit.

I told him I was writing this book and asked permission to jot his story down. My notes are reproduced below:

> I did my own tax returns, but I kept every receipt. I had detailed records. The IRS just destroyed my business. They audited me and said I owed them $47 thousand. That was more than I made in a year. I just couldn't stand that kind of abuse.

> The agent was abusive and rude. It became apparent from the very beginning that he was out to get me. I felt like the Gestapo had me! I will never deal with the IRS again.

So, I sold my business and purchased this rig. I went on the road as an itinerant blacksmith. On a good day, at a fair or trade-day, I can make $500. I only make $20 thousand to $25 thousand a year, all tax free. I don't pay the IRS a dime. I don't file returns and I'm not going to start. Those e——— IRS agents will never get another dime from me!

This type of story is all too common. Mr. Blacksmith made three serious errors. He did his own tax return. He tried to represent himself in an IRS audit. And, he allowed other people and circumstances to turn him from an honest taxpayer into a tax cheat. He is a tax cheat, not a tax protester.

I do not doubt this man's story. He had no reason to lie. The IRS may have appeared to him abusive. IRS agents get really frustrated with a disorganized mess. Routinely, IRS agents will refuse to look through a mess of jumbled papers. To a man already nervous and frightened of what he does not understand, that may appear abusive. I get along with IRS agents very well. When I do work on an IRS examination, my work is well organized and well presented. IRS agents appreciate such effort because it helps them do their job.

Case Study: The Christian Shopkeeper

My wife, Jane, surprised me for my fortieth birthday. She planned a trip to one of our favorite retreats in the mountains of Georgia. We like to buy mountain crafts for gifts, so we visit a lot of craft shops.

In one shop I saw a sign that said, "Make all checks payable to cash." Once I established that the shopkeeper was a Christian (I always talk about Jesus and business), I asked about the sign. My notes are reproduced below:

"I don't take credit cards either. I will leave nothing for the IRS to trace. I don't pay taxes. I have never paid taxes. I will not give those e——— IRS people the time of day."

I asked if the IRS had ever done him any harm, he said no. "How could they, they do not even know I exist."

This gentlemen is not a tax protestor. He is a tax cheat. Believe it or not, the IRS has ways of finding him too.

Endnotes

1. Love gifts paid to a pastor are almost always fully taxable.

2. I heard the legendary lawyer David Gibbs give this definition in a 1983 speech in Atlanta, Georgia.

3. See Matthew 9:10–11, 11:19, 21:31–32; Mark 2:15–16; and Luke 3:12, 5:29, 5:30, 7:29, 7:34, 15:1.

CHAPTER SIX

Our Fears:
IRS Attacks the Church

Christian Political Activities Pay Off

The good news is that political pressure from Christians angry about federal tax policy pays off. For the first time in American history, on 1 January 1984, the Church became subject to mandatory federal taxation by being forced into the Social Security system. Many churches were angry about this abrupt change in federal tax policy.

Many of our Christian leaders envisioned massive IRS invasions of the Church on the pretext of auditing Social Security and payroll records. In 1984, the new police powers granted to the IRS by the Bob Jones case were fresh on everyone's mind and a source of deep concern. The fear was of random IRS fishing trips looking for possible violations of tax law. The presumption was that the IRS would be anxious to exercise their new "Bob Jones" police powers.

Church Audit Procedures Act

Leaders in the Christian movement mounted a political protest to Congress. This protest was legal and courteous. Congressmen were approached directly and by mail. The Church's concerns were expressed. We politely reminded our nation's legislators that Christians vote, and angry Christians vote in big blocks. Incidentally, this is what the IRS today would call political campaign activities, and most likely rule illegal.

This responsible and democratic pressure applied to Congress had several positive results. One was to have an accommodation written into tax law allowing certain churches to exempt out of direct Social Security taxation. However, the main benefit of this Christian led political movement is the 1983 Church Audit Procedures Act. The act makes direct audits of churches much more difficult and outlaws any IRS "fishing expeditions" inside churches.

I am being intentionally vague about the provisions of the Church Audit Act. If your church ever receives a notification of an IRS audit, I recommend, in the strongest possible terms, you hire a CPA or a lawyer with recent church tax law experience. Please do not ever try to exercise your legal rights before the IRS on your own. It could prove to be a devastating mistake.

Dealing with the IRS on any audit is like walking into a lion's den. If you must go, walk behind a lion tamer. A good lawyer or a good CPA can serve the lion tamer function before the IRS. A lawyer or a CPA will not win your audit for you. You win or lose an IRS audit on the facts. The only things a good lawyer or CPA can accomplish for you before the IRS is to see that your rights are not violated and to help you present your facts in the most complete manner possible. When you or your church stands before the IRS, presenting the facts is your job. It is not the responsibility of the IRS. They will not help you present your facts.

The IRS Expressed Concern

For obvious reasons the IRS had reservations about the 1983 Church Audit Act. The Treasury's assistant secretary for tax policy at the time, Ronald A. Pearlman, expressed concern that the act "would serve only to insulate tax protesters and sham churches from legitimate IRS investigation." Via Mr. Pearlman's efforts, many of the restrictions limiting IRS power over churches were modified or toned down.

In spite of being diminished, the Church Audit Act accomplished its purpose of limited IRS audits and "fishing expeditions" inside of churches.

As a result of the Church Audit Act, it is now harder for the IRS to audit a church than any other tax-exempt organization. Therefore, very few churches are audited.

In 1983, the IRS made two startling revelations. In the three preceding fiscal years, the IRS audited 116 churches. On average, thirty-eight or thirty-nine churches were being audited each year. In the same announcement, the IRS also revealed that it had an inventory of fifteen thousand open cases involving returns associated with alleged tax avoidance schemes.[1] I am sure a significant portion of these fifteen thousand were tax protesters.

Ten years later, the July/August issue of *Church Law and Tax Report,* edited by Richard R. Hammar, reported that there are probably less than ten churches per year that lose their tax-exempt status.[2] Most of these ten churches would be tax shams. As a direct result of the 1983 Church Audit Act we have fewer direct audits of churches today than we did ten years ago. This legislation has been effective.

Although actual IRS audits of churches have fallen off sharply due to the Church Audit Act, IRS activities involving churches have sharply increased. Audits are not the only IRS method of policing churches.

Church Tax Inquiries

One change caused by the Church Audit Act is a new IRS tool called a church tax inquiry, which is not an audit and is therefore not subject to the same restrictions.[3] It is very much like an audit but just enough different that the IRS is allowed to bypass the restrictions on church audits.

Before a church tax inquiry can begin, an IRS official must reasonably believe that the church does not qualify for tax-exempt status.[4] A church's failure to respond to "routine information" gives the IRS authority to begin a church tax inquiry.[5]

An IRS tax inquiry is supposedly less in scope than an IRS audit, but it can still challenge the tax-exempt status of a church.[6] Based upon a simple tax inquiry, the IRS may discover facts and circumstances outside the scope of the initial tax inquiry. The IRS is then allowed to explore these new facts. If a complaint is made to the IRS about possible improprieties or if other information comes to the attention of the IRS about possible violations of law, it can trigger a church tax inquiry. The IRS is also not required to tell you what evidence they have or to identify their sources of information.[7] In tax law, the accused has no right to face his accusers.

In either a church audit or a church tax inquiry there are three important matters that the IRS can look into:

1. church membership and contributions lists.[8]

2. letters and other communications between clergy and church members. Unlike criminal law, tax law has no concept of confidential and privileged communications between clergy and church members.

3. the religious practices of the church to the extent necessary to verify the organization's status as a church.[9]

Many people believe that the items on this list represent dangerous and unconstitutional powers of the IRS over churches. Attorney David Gibbs, a nationally renowned expert in church legal matters, cited this list in 1983 at Temple Baptist Church in Atlanta.

The church tax inquiry is a strange IRS creature, a sort of non-audit audit. I know that sounds like a contradiction in terms, but as I have said before, there is little logic to tax law. Even with the big loopholes punched into the Church Audit Act by the church tax inquiry, there are yet other methods around the intent of this law.

Exceptions to Church Audit Rules

Routine requests by the IRS are not restricted by the Church Audit Act. David Allison, formerly head of our firm's Church Services Division, calls these routine requests "informal audits." Typical examples of routine requests are

1. any information concerning a church's full compliance with tax withholdings and Social Security rules and all required information returns (IRS Form W-2 or Form 1099).

2. any information needed to process an application for exempt status and a request for a private letter ruling.

3. any information needed by the IRS necessary to update the Cumulative List of Tax-Exempt Organizations, IRS Publication 78, also called the Blue Book.

4. any information as to whether or not a specific business enterprise is owned or operated by a church.[10]

5. cases involving civil tax fraud, criminal investigations, nonfilers and tax protestors.[11]

6. any records held by banks and other third parties are exempt from the Church Audit Act. The IRS can examine these records without restrictions. In addition, a church is required to assist the IRS in locating and examining any third party records. Unlike criminal, civil, and other types of American law, a taxpayer has no Fifth Amendment protections against self-incrimination.

7. Church Audit Act procedures also do not apply to IRS examinations concerning assignments of income, services, or contributions to a church.

8. Finally, tax inquiries or audits that primarily concern the pastor, church staff, or other taxpayers are also exempt from the procedures under the Church Audit Act.

In my experience, there has been a virtual explosion of IRS activities in churches that fall under the routine requests exceptions to the law. The most common of these IRS invasions are payroll tax problems (listed as item number 1 above) and inquiries or audits or third parties (listed as item number 8 above). The IRS does not publish this data; however, my educated guess is that over one hundred thousand routine requests are made by the IRS to churches each year.

In 1988, the IRS computers began tracking down all ministers who reported their income and expenses on Schedule C. Thousands of IRS notices were then sent to ministers requesting modest amounts of additional taxes, normally two hundred dollar to five hundred dollar amounts. A protest by a minister quickly evolved into the IRS making routine requests for supporting compensation records of churches.

Requesting a minister's compensation records from a church is a routine request because the primary concern of the IRS is not the church but the minister. Payroll and payroll tax problems have generated the vast majority of the IRS's routine requests.

Endnotes

1. *Tax Notes,* 17 October 1983.

2. Mathews, N.C., "Christian Ministry Resources," *Church Law and Tax Report* (July/August): 1995.

3. IRC S 7611(h)(2).

4. IRC S 7611(a)(2), (h)(7).

5. Reg S 301.7611-1, Q & A 7.

6. Staff of the Joint Committee on Taxation, General Explanation of the Deficit Reduction Act of 1984, 98th Cong, 2d Sess 1141, 1984.

7. Reg S 301.7611-1, Q & A 9.

8. The IRS has, in the past, exercised its power to audit lists of the contributors to various tax-exempt organizations. That would probably dry up the cash-flow! In fact, that is exactly what the IRS intended to do in these extreme cases, put errant tax-exempt organizations out of business.

9. IRC S 7611(h)(3).

10. Reg S 301.7611-1, Q & A 4

11. IRC S 7611(i); Reg S 301.7611-1, Q & As 6, 8.

CHAPTER SEVEN

Responsibilities:
The Power of the IRS to Audit

True excellence in ministry is uncommon. I am blessed. A disproportionately large number of these uncommonly excellent ministries are my clients. These ministries believe our CPA firm helps them, and they are grateful for what we do. The real blessing is all mine. To see what some of these extraordinary ministries accomplish leaves me speechless. To protect such ministries from official abuse is my most satisfying professional activity.

One of the most unsettling cases in which I was the primary CPA involved an excellent ministry accused by the IRS of exercising free speech. The IRS interpreted this organization's speech to be political, not moral or spiritual. I saw a situation firsthand where the charge of exercising free speech could mean the loss of a ministry of the kingdom of God. The experience left me badly shaken.

We should be beating the drums and singing their praises in the media, yet our society is determined to ignore the good they do in the name of Jesus. The lack of recognition and the lack of gratitude for these excellent ministries is symptomatic of the harsh judgment of society against the Church. Even when these ministries make important contributions for the benefit of our entire nation, gratitude is very rare.

Without a doubt one of the most excellent ministries I have ever been associated with as a CPA spent most of 1992 fighting for its life with the IRS. I will refer to it as Pray for Peace Ministries.

For reasons that will become obvious in this chapter, the identity of this ministry must remain confidential.

This was a full IRS audit of a church. From the point of view of the IRS, Pray for Peace was probably not a church. However, we will let you decide if this ministry is, or is not, a part of the Church in America.

Pray for Peace Ministries was born out of a powerful vision from God to a wonderful woman, alias Mrs. Ima N. Faith. Ima is a gifted business woman who became financially independent through her own efforts, and her vision came after years devoted to prayer and Bible study.

This was no quick decision. It was a careful consideration of the way God moved Mrs. Faith's heart. Ima shared with me her belief that any Christian could gain a vision from God the same way she did, spending significant time in prayer and Bible study. Once, Mrs. Faith said to me, "God is waiting and willing to communicate with his people if only we will humble ourselves and pray." To Mrs. Faith, prayer is not five to ten minutes of mumbling. Prayer is more thoughtful and better planned. It is not taking time out of your day so much as it is a way of life.

This young ministry was formed a bit less than ten years ago. From the very beginning, the founder made a commitment to financial integrity and excellence that is extraordinary. I find it somewhat amusing that United Way and other national nonprofit organizations have new and highly touted Codes of Ethics after being exposed to national disgrace. The Codes of Ethics for Pray for Peace Ministries was in place before the first day of business. It has been strictly adhered to ever since.

From the very first day, the Code of Ethics in place at this ministry was extraordinary. The financial controls were to be established by a well-known national CPA firm. The original by-laws and organization were written by a lawyer with ministry experience. The IRS was allowed to review the organizational documents and financial controls before granting tax- exempt status. At least once each year CPAs and lawyers were consulted on matters of financial integrity and control. Ima planned to be excellent from the very beginning.

To avoid even the hint of personal gain, the top officers agreed to work without any compensation. Two officers still work full time with no pay whatsoever. These two officers are also substantial contributors to the ministry.

Fundraising and administrative costs were intentionally minimized by having most of the work done by volunteers. Money is carefully and thoughtfully committed to ministry after much prayer. The level of efficiency achieved can only be described as amazing. Of all the money that comes into the ministry, over 85 percent goes directly into the mission. Less than 15 percent is spent on fundraising and administrative costs. This is truly an excellent ministry.

This level of ethical conduct and financial integrity did not happen by accident. This ministry was given by God to a willing servant.

The process followed by Mrs. Ima N. Faith seems obvious and logical. It is! Yet, it is also unusual in the Church. Most Christian ministries seem to skip over the hard stuff like ethics and financial planning. Before his fall, the infamous preacher Jim Bakker was quoted as saying, "Don't listen to accountants and lawyers. They will kill your vision." That attitude caused Mr. Bakker to go to prison. Unfortunately, the Jim Bakker attitude is too common in the Church today.

Mrs. Faith committed herself to following God. She was totally devoted to her vision, yet dedicated to the highest standards of ethical and financial conduct. Mrs. Faith's high standards required the assistance of lawyers and CPAs.

Intense prayer seems to bear consistent and predicable results for different people. God giving consistent leadership to his people should not surprise us.

Pray for Peace Ministries is similar to other excellent ministries in that they focus on the real needs of people. They have seven primary ministries that are clearly ministries of hope:

1. Family welfare relief
2. Back to school clothing for the poor
3. Power and utility bills paid in times of crisis
4. Home repairs for the poor
5. Prison ministry

6. The education ministry
7. The ministry of prayer

Pray for Peace Ministries also has an overwhelming commitment to civil rights, the rights of the poor, positive relationships between the white and black communities, and a conviction of faith that before God there can be no distinctions based upon race. To quote Mrs. Ima N. Faith, "There is no black or white, rich or poor, slave or free before God. There are only the children of faith and the lost."

The social problems to which Pray for Peace Ministries is dedicated are based upon conservative Christian doctrines and the deep-seated belief that the government should not be involved in these ministries. Mrs. Faith and I share one belief: we believe the government is part of the problem not part of the solution. If we have a solution to these perplexing problems, it must come from the private sector and a huge investment must come from the Church.

Foreign Missions, A Ministry to Russia

Like Paul's dream that led him to a ministry in Europe, the post-Cold War opportunities in Russia cannot be ignored. Following the leadership of God to bring a ministry of hope to Russia, Pray for Peace Ministries established a mission on foreign soil.

Precisely the same pattern was followed: the best lawyers with international ministry experience were hired; local Russian lawyers were hired; and, the best CPAs were consulted—all with the single aim of insuring the same high level of ethics and integrity that are the well-known trademarks of Pray for Peace Ministries. The local Russian authorities reviewed and approved the ministry's application for official Russian recognition.

To some degree, the Russian ministry follows the same pattern as the American ministry. Pray for Peace Ministries provides eight basic ministries to Russia:

1. Family welfare
2. Russia's youth
3. Medical supplies and medicines
4. The ministry of the Word
5. The ministry of prayer

6. Soup kitchens
7. Kindergartens
8. Prison ministry

Is This Really a Church?

I proudly proclaim that Pray for Peace Ministries is indeed a part of the Church in America. They meet to worship weekly in prayer and the Word of God. Their ministries are exceptional in scope. Their ethics and financial integrity are beyond question. Until the IRS showed up to audit the books, Mrs. Ima N. Faith thought Pray for Peace Ministries was a part of the American Church.

The IRS's Definition of a Church

Unfortunately, the IRS may not see Pray for Peace Ministries as a church. The IRS has a strange, somewhat twisted, fourteen-point definition of a church:

1. A legal existence
2. An officially recognized creed and form of worship
3. A distinct ecclesiastical government
4. A code of doctrine and discipline
5. A distinct religious history
6. A membership not associated with another church
7. An organization of ordained ministers
8. Ordained ministers serving after completing a prescribed course of study
9. A distinct religious literature
10. Established place of worship
11. Regular congregation
12. Regular religious services
13. Sunday schools and other training events
14. School for ministerial preparation

Pray for Peace Ministries may not be a church by the IRS's definition. Item number 6, "A membership not associated with another church," would be a problem given that most of their weekly worshipers are ministers themselves. And, items 11 through 14 might be difficult as well. Their worship is primarily mid-week, not the traditional Sunday day of worship.

These fourteen points define a church from the viewpoint of the IRS. The IRS's view of a church is a nice little building on the corner where people go twice on Sunday and maybe once on Wednesday. In other words, the IRS wants a church to be traditional. New movements in Christ and intensive investments in social ministries do not fit well into the IRS's narrow definition.

What Is a Church Anyway?

Is Pray for Peace Ministries a church by this fourteen-point definition? I don't know. If I had been unable to reach a reasonable compromise with the IRS during the service's audit of Pray for Peace Ministries, I would have alleged a violation of the Church Audit Act and taken the IRS to court to find out.

Before a jury, I honestly do not know how they would rule. We could put many civil rights leaders from over a dozen states on the witness stand to testify to the faith and practice of Pray for Peace Ministries. We would have a compelling case. However, I am thankful this case did not go to court. A gamble in court could easily cost this nation one of her prized assets, the Pray for Peace Ministries.

To me, a church is any organization that unites together for prayer, worship, and to meet the call of Christ. A narrow, government-sponsored definition is almost a heresy. I believe with all my heart that Pray for Peace Ministries is a part of my Church.

Howard M. Schoenfeld, a top IRS official in the area of tax-exempt organizations, and Richard R. Hammar, J.D., LL.M., CPA, one of the nation's leading authorities on legal and tax matters of churches, both contend that church audits are rare. They may be rare according to the narrow IRS definition of a church. However, Pray for Peace Ministries spent much of 1992 going through a bitter audit.

Pray for Peace Ministries has two important missions: education and prayer. The two go hand in hand—education and wisdom, prayer and healing. These ministries unite to inform the Church of important issues in our society and lead the Church to pray for these issues. The initial documents prepared by lawyers and approved by the IRS clearly state these missions. Mrs. Faith's convictions are that without knowledge there can be no wisdom and no vision from God. It is only by the humility of prayer can our nation be healed.

Early in the 1980s, Pray for Peace Ministries became alarmed at the growing trend to legitimize homosexual behavior in our society. Newsletters, books, and tapes were devoted to the topic all with one consistent conclusion: pray. Education and prayer, consistently for many years, was the key mission of this organization.

It was a part of their mission when they were first audited in 1986. That audit went very smoothly. The agent was cordial and friendly. But, by 1992, things had changed in our society. The homosexual lobby's power-base was larger, and the impact of homosexuals on national politics was more pronounced. The 1992 IRS audit of Pray for Peace Ministries was triggered by the education and prayer missions of the organization.

A newsletter was issued devoted to the growing power of homosexuals in our nation's politics. This newsletter was very offensive to homosexuals, but it was not intended for homosexuals to read; it was intended for the evangelical Christian community. Pray for Peace Ministries and I have reason to believe that a liberal preacher objected to the discussion and turned them into the IRS. This particular newsletter focused on the long prohomosexual history of a certain presidential candidate

Pray for Peace Ministries received a telephone call from an IRS agent informing them that they were being audited for the years 1989 to 1991. The staff was told on what day Mr. Agent planned to arrive. Neither Mrs. Ima N. Faith nor the senior staff of Pray for Peace Ministries were alarmed. In 1986 they went through a very thorough audit by the IRS with no problems whatsoever. In fact, the 1986 IRS agent was very helpful making various suggestions to improve accounting and reporting over the sale of books and tapes. The only problem was that all the senior staff had already scheduled a trip to Russia (a complex process not easily altered). The agent was called back and told this day was inconvenient and to please reschedule.

Once back in the states, the staff again called to reschedule the audit. While in Russia, the entire senior staff got sick. They were physically not able to make the meeting. The IRS agent was verbally unhappy about this inconvenience. Yet, a third time the agent was called to reschedule the trip due to the fact that one of the illnesses had progressed to serious. This time the agent was verbally abusive. Apparently, he did not believe Pray for Peace Ministries was being truthful.

From the very first, this audit got off on a wrong foot. To the senior staff, the IRS agent seemed to have an I'm-gonna-get-you attitude. The CPA doing the initial field work told Mrs. Faith that, while looking over certain records, the agent exclaimed, "I've got you now!" Obviously, this IRS agent was becoming too personally involved in this case. Unlike the 1986 audit, there was no effort to be fair, concerned, or helpful. The IRS in this case was bent upon punishing Pray for Peace Ministries. This was far more than a mere personality conflict; this attitude represented an official change in IRS policy.

This attitude was new and unexpected. IRS agents in commercial audits are normally fair and friendly. An inexperienced CPA allowed herself to be intimidated. She was terrified. At one point, she told Mrs. Faith that the Pray for Peace Ministries may owe the IRS $250,000 or more!

The IRS agent did not believe that Mrs. Faith worked so hard for no compensation and tried diligently to establish that she was receiving some personal benefits from Pray for Peace Ministries. The exhaustive work of the IRS produced no financial irregularities or problems whatsoever. However, based on the newsletter about homosexuals, the IRS agent proposed to revoke the tax-exempt status of Pray for Peace Ministries.

The hazard of revocation was a dire threat. For the first time, Mrs. Faith and the senior staff of Pray for Peace realized that their wonderful ministries may be lost to the kingdom of God! This fact and its full implications were difficult for all the people associated with Pray for Peace Ministries to comprehend. The people who would be hurt the most would be the poorest citizens. Thousands of people would suffer!

The physical and emotional costs of this threat to Mrs. Faith was overwhelming. Even her personality changed under this harassment.

The IRS agent made it very plain that he intended to revoke Pray for Peace Ministries. Mrs. Ima N. Faith's family tax lawyer agreed to take the case. Mr. Lawyer is a battle-scarred old veteran in the tax wars. However, like me and most other tax professionals, he was not prepared for this IRS onslaught.

Part of the problem that most CPAs and lawyers have in dealing with nonprofit audits is that IRS procedures are radically different in this arena. In a common audit of a commercial business, the agent comes in and does an audit with the assistance of the taxpayer and the CPA. After the audit, the agent writes a report proposing assessments of tax. Then, the fun begins. We get to talk to the agent's supervisor to negotiate a compromise or maybe file a letter of protest and request an appellant level conference. At the appellant level, the appeals officer will often negotiate a compromise or refer the case back to the field if necessary. The appeals officer and the CPA or tax lawyer may disagree, and the IRS assesses the additional tax as "unagreed."

Unagreed cases that cannot be resolved within the IRS often go to one of various courts, Tax Court and U.S. District Court are the most common. If you elect to go to Tax Court, you do not have to pay any taxes until the court issues its ruling on your case. Of course, interest is accumulating all the time the appeal process continues. In U.S. District Court the taxpayer must first pay the tax and petition the court for a refund. My personal tax lawyer, Bruce P. Ely, tells me that a lot of legal maneuvering and planning goes into selecting the correct court.

In a nonprofit tax audit these rules are radically different. The IRS field agent's report is much harder to modify once issued in a nonprofit audit. Compromise negotiations with the field agent's supervisor and with the IRS's appellate level are much more difficult than commercial audits. A proposed revocation of tax-exempt status becomes nearly automatic. Unaware of these peculiar procedures, Mr. Lawyer did not involve himself in the day-to-day audit process leaving that to a CPA he knew to be inexperienced. Under normal conditions, the day-to-day work of representing a client to the IRS in the field is traditionally a CPA's function. Lawyers often stay out of the field work but jump into the fray when legal maneuvering and planning become important.

As the field audit began to wind down, the IRS agent and the family tax lawyer met on several occasions. The IRS agent wanted to know how the lawyer was going to respond to these charges that Pray for Peace Ministries was involved in political campaign activities. Mr. Lawyer replied that he had seen no charges and that he would respond to written charges. The IRS agent insisted that he didn't want to issue the report.

Mr. Lawyer, totally unaware of procedural differences in nonprofit audits, wanted to know how he can respond to charges that are not written down! The lawyer was so immersed in commercial tax audit procedures that he failed to understand the IRS agent's threat to issue this report. The IRS agent, on the other hand, was completely aware of how serious the mere act of issuing a report may prove to be and would like to resolve the situation without a report. This miscommunication allowed a report to be issued, a report that neither the IRS nor Pray for Peace Ministries wanted.

Mr. Lawyer planned to review the charges and make an appointment with the IRS agent's supervisor. With the supervisor, the lawyer was going to point out violations of the Church Audit Procedure Act and have the case referred back to the field. With the charges in hand, the lawyer believed he could have the IRS reaudit Pray for Peace Ministries and have the political charges eliminated. He and everybody else associated with the Pray for Peace Ministries sincerely believed these charges to be bogus. He soon realized his error.

After the report was issued, the agent wouldn't talk to him. The agent said the report closed the case, and the supervisor wouldn't even talk to the lawyer. The report was sent to Atlanta for the IRS's quality review. The lawyers who work for the IRS would verify the political charges based upon the field agent's report and, most likely, recommend revocation.

Once the IRS internally makes a decision to revoke, the revocation becomes automatic! From the day the IRS publishes notice of revocation in the Federal Register forward, contributions to Pray for Peace Ministries would not have been tax deductible. Pray for Peace Ministries would have died!

The right of the IRS to summarily revoke the status of a tax-exempt organization without prior judicial review has recently been restated by the courts in a 1993 case.[2] That is not necessarily the end of the legal battle; however, it is clear that an organization is unlikely to survive an IRS revocation.

This case had spiraled out of control, and the implications of the case were rapidly becoming apparent. In the middle of this horrendous process, the lawyer's health failed. And, the lawyer was not the only person to succumb to stress-related illnesses. Due to the stress of the audit, two of the principal operating officers also became seriously ill.

From his hospital, the lawyer called and asked me if I would take over the case. The first line of defense had failed.

To be frank, I was not a whole lot better prepared than Mr. Lawyer. Like him, I have not been through an aggressive audit of a nonprofit organization. Although I have been through a number of nonprofit tax audits, I never experienced an adverse tax determination and certainly not a threat of revocation!

I faxed my power of attorney form to the field agent and requested he call me. No response. I refaxed the material; still no response. The agent refused to call me. I called him and asked him why he wouldn't call me, and he told me the case was out of his hands. It had been sent to quality review in Atlanta. As far as he was concerned, the case was closed.

I asked him how the case could be closed, since we haven't even responded to the charges. That's when I learned about the unique procedures for exempt organization audits. The agent told me he was sorry, but the case was out of his hands.

I asked the agent how I could get the case reopened only to be told that I couldn't. I asked the agent if I could discuss the case with his supervisor, to which he responded, "My supervisor has already reviewed the case before it was sent to quality review." Finally, the agent agreed to give me the name and telephone number of his supervisor in Atlanta. By this time, I was getting plenty nervous.

I faxed my power of attorney to the supervisor and called him on the telephone only to be told the same thing. The case had already gone to quality review. He couldn't get it back. I told him we hadn't had a chance to respond to the charges, and Mr. Supervisor told me, "They had a CPA and lawyer in the field." I tried to explain to Mr. Supervisor that neither they nor I understood the IRS's process in these cases. The initial attitude is "not much I can do."

I pointed out that Mrs. Faith is financially independent and well able to fight this matter in court and that her well-known commitment to civil rights would allow us an impressive group of nationally known civil rights leaders as witnesses to discuss Pray for Peace Ministries' investment in the community. His attention was mildly sparked, but I confess very mildly.

I asked him if he would like to see our response to the charges. I had previously written a letter of protest in a two column format—the agent's report was in the left-hand column and Pray for Peace Ministries' response was in the right. Mr. Supervisor guessed he might like to see that response. I printed off two of these lengthy protest letters and express-mailed them, one to Mr. Supervisor and one to the field agent.

After a day or two to allow Mr. Supervisor to review my work, I called him again. He was mildly impressed with my letter, but I confess very mildly. After a protracted discussion, Mr. Supervisor agreed to try and retrieve the case from the quality review staff. One thing worked in our favor: the IRS's quality review staff was three or four months behind in their workload, and they probably wouldn't mind letting me have this case back.

These negotiations with Mr. Supervisor were friendly, honest, and professional. In my opinion, that is the only productive way to deal with the IRS. If I had approached Mr. Supervisor as a wild-eyed fanatic out for his blood, this case would never have been reopened. I have repeated this statement over and over again in the book, but it is important to remember, "The IRS is not our enemy!"

Praise God, Mr. Supervisor got the case back and agreed to reopen the field work. The case was sent back to the field agent, and I began my negotiations with him.

My letter of protest shot big holes in major parts of the field agent's report, but there was one inescapable fact hanging heavy over the whole case: even one instant of a confirmed political activity is all that is required for revocation. The entire argument came down to the newsletter devoted to the presidential candidate's prohomosexual politics.

Even now, I still believe this newsletter was not a political campaign effort. Given the long history of education and calling the nation to pray over social issues, I believe this newsletter is a call to prayer. Eighteen times in a three-page article, Mrs. Faith calls for prayer. Never once did she tell people how to vote. In fact, she affirmatively said, "It is not the intent of this newsletter to tell you how to vote, but how to pray."

Pray for Peace was organized to call America back to prayer for a revival of Christianity: back to its roots, back to its moorings.

Excerpts from the Newsletter

Only God can move mountains, but prayer dictates which one He moves. As Christians we should earnestly desire and pray for the salvation of ————. Let us unceasingly pray for "all that are in authority," 1 Timothy 2:2, Romans 13:1.

And since prayer is the only power on earth that commands the power of heaven, join in this symphony of supplication that God will give to our beloved America in every office up for election in November, only men and women whose record indicates they are dedicated to Godly principles; to preservation of our Christian heritage, and to the strengthening of our Christian influence.

Take this newsletter with you to church, Sunday School, prayer meeting, to school, to eat, to work, and inform your friends of facts, not fiction or gossip. Never have I been so burdened to pray about a political issue. When my anguish is over political concerns, then I must pray, speak and write, even as Jeremiah did.

If Christians do not wake up now, join hands, work, pray and inform others of this impending catastrophe, I predict a Cultural Revolution, not unlike that imposed on the Chinese in the 1960's which saw 80 million Christians murdered, Bibles confiscated and churches burned.

Form prayer Watch Committees in the churches, and pray for God to divinely intervene, and mercifully grant to us men and women dedicated to Godly principles in every office on the ballot.

Pray also that God will confound the enemy camps, confuse their plans, perplex their strategists and order good out of this planned evil. Pray also for me, that God will open a door of utterance, and that I will boldly declare the truth, being unmoved at people's faces, and diminishing not a word; and also, that God will preserve me; spirit, soul and body blameless; that he will hedge me in, hide me in his pavilion, and be a wall of fire about me—in my uprising and my downsitting, my going out and my coming in.

I have read this newsletter a thousand times, and I am still convinced that if we went to court we could win. But, the price of going to court to win a constitutional issue is too high. Pray for Peace Ministries would have been put out of business. A three-to five-year court fight with no contributions coming into the ministry would have destroyed Pray for Peace Ministries.

In my opinion, the IRS was really abusive in this case. They took full advantage of their nearly unlimited power to retroactively revoke an organization's tax exemption in an effort to silence an important voice in our society's debate over morality.

Based upon this power, they took positions that are wrong and unreasonable. First, it is clear, and the agent and agent supervisor conceded, that Mrs. Faith never intended to be actively engaged in political campaign activities. Their position was that intent is not required. I simply do not believe it is possible to be actively engaged in political campaign activities without intending to do so. The IRS's position on the issue of intent is filled with internal contradictions. A good lawyer would have a field day in court exploring these contradictions. Second, the IRS defined "political campaign activities" in the field to include the mere mention of a political candidate by name or even the mention of members of a political candidate's family by name in a noncampaign context.

For example, Neal Bush, former President George Bush's son, had some unfortunate financial dealings with a failed Savings & Loan. The mere mention of this was a political campaign activity though no mention was made of George or politics. On this point the agent got more than a little extreme.

A brief section of my letter of protest follows:

In fact you listed the following six men as being a target of these alleged negative campaign activities: Governor ————, President George Bush, Gorbachev, Marcos, Neal Bush, Jeb Bush.

Of the six men you list in your report as targets of "negative campaign activities," four are not candidates for any United States political office. What legal significance does Gorbachev and Marcos have to a 501 (c)(3) organization? Why are they even mentioned in your report?

I fail to see how even the nonpolitical mention of a nonpolitical person could be construed as "political campaign activities."

The IRS never backed down, retracted, or modified their opinions, even in the face of what I believe to be convincing evidence. The unrestrained power to revoke gives them this leverage. You can't beat them, and they know it all too well.

But, we did have a convincing case and a woman determined to go to court to protect what she believes is a ministry that belongs to God.[3] Of course, that large group of nationally known civil rights leaders, willing to testify as to the effectiveness of the ministry, had a modest impact as well. We reached a compromise agreement.

In our compromise settlement, Pray for Peace Ministries agreed to sign a closing statement in which they promised to refrain from political campaign activities in the future. They also agreed to pay a modest fine. Pray for Peace Ministries gladly signed the agreement. The alternative was to forfeit one of the Lord's most effective ministries. The only problem is that we still do not believe Pray for Peace Ministries engaged in any political activities. However, we signed just so we can "live at peace with all men" (Rom. 12:18), even the IRS.

The tax cost was nowhere near the frightened cost estimate of $250,000. We paid a modest fine of $2,819 for these alleged "political activities." With all interest charges, the total came to $3,519.

I recently spoke to the agent, and he assured me that the closing letter will be coming soon. The only problem is that the IRS computers do not know how to record receipt of these fines for "political activities." Once they can straighten out their computers, the closing letter will be on its way. I asked him if the IRS had a lot of cases like this in process, to which he said, "I'm covered up."

This was the most technically demanding and emotionally draining experience of my professional life. No one should have to go through what Mrs. Ima N. Faith and Pray for Peace Ministries were subjected to. The medical bills alone due to stress-related illnesses cost more that the modest fines. It is a tragedy, but it could have been a much greater tragedy.

The simple conclusion is that our federal government has decided to eliminate all politically sensitive discussions by conservative Christian organizations at the same time that moderate organizations are actually encouraged to participate in election activities. You will never hear of a moderate Christian or charitable organization being charged with "political activities"—never, although records of true and effective political activities abound.

The black Baptist group, the National Baptist Association, will never be charged with political activities for publicly endorsing a candidate for mayor of New York, nor should they be. But, neither should more conservative Christian movements. The phrase itself, "political activities," as a legal charge against anyone, has a repulsive sound to it, an un-American sound. The IRS has no legitimate place policing political free speech whatsoever! This misuse of the IRS by Congress indicates the pitiful low to which our tax code has sunk.

I believe it is clear that our country needs serious tax reforms, not just in the not-for-profit sector either. Our nation's tax and fiscal policies are on the edge of spinning out of control and threaten our economy. These policies are already squeezing the middle class into poverty. We need reforms that will rein in the power of the IRS and remove tax-imposed retrains on economic growth. Such reforms will ignite the growth of the middle class. When the middle class grows, poverty begins to heal.

Endnotes

1. In May of 1992, the IRS made a public commitment to take all Christian organizations out of the political process.

2. *United Cancer council, Inc., v. Commr,* 100 TC No 11 (1993). In 1969 the United Cancer Council received a favorable ruling on its exempt status. In 1990 the service revoked this exemption retroactively to 1984. The organization went to court seeking a declaratory judgment, asking for summary judgment on the grounds that revocation without a prior judicial hearing violated its rights to procedural due process. In denying the organization's request, the tax court relied in part on the opinion in the 1974 pre-IRC Section 7428 case of *Bob Jones University v. Simon,* 416 US 725 (1974).

3. The IRS believes that all ministries, by virtue of being tax exempt, belong to the people. This difference in attitude may be the root of our problems!

CHAPTER EIGHT

Reforms:
The Reagan-Kennedy Revolution

The title of this chapter, "The Reagan-Kennedy Revolution," seems like sacrilege to both liberals and conservatives alike. Most Americans think Presidents Ronald Reagan and John F. Kennedy have little in common. They are wrong.

Liberals look on Reagan as a malignant, menacing, and sinister president. But, most conservatives are more kind to John Kennedy. They merely say Kennedy was a bad president and point to the Bay of Pigs fiasco, the use of assassination as a tool of foreign policy, mismanaged foreign policy that brought the world to the brink of a nuclear holocaust, and the escalation of the Vietnam War as examples.

Even though conservatives are generally more kind to Kennedy, the liberals vehemently despise Reagan. Forgetting the tremendous burden of social spending programs inherited from Lyndon Johnson's failed Great American Dream, they point to military build-up as the cause of mounting deficits. They believe that Reagan led the nation to retreat on civil rights issues, ignoring the fact that black families made significant economic strides under his leadership and that spending on social programs aimed at black families actually increased during his administration. They say that Reagan was not intellectually equipped to be president. That old-fashioned Hamilton-Federalist elitism pops up again!

They even accuse Reagan of selective memory loss. Well, they may have a point on this one. I never said liberals were stupid. I only implied that some of them are mean. As it turns out, Reagan's selective memory loss may have been the early stages of Alzheimer's.

Interestingly, Presidents Ronald Reagan and John F. Kennedy have much in common. They were both honest and patriotic men; neither tried to hide his political views or policy agenda from America; and they were both leaders in an important American political "revolution": Reagan's revolution was in economics, and Kennedy's revolution was in civil rights. And, even with their significant accomplishments, both fell short of their personal goals for our nation.

These were great men, worthy of the honor of joining the American debate that has defined our nation's heritage and our current freedoms. These men are of the same mold as some of America's greatest men: Hamilton, Jefferson, Lincoln, William Jennings Bryan, and so many more. I am proud they were American leaders. Our nation is richer because of them.

The assassination of President Kennedy in November of 1963 broke my heart. These many years later, I mourn that America was robbed of one of her greatest patriots. I can't help but grieve for what he could have accomplished; he was cut down too young.

When Reagan was shot, I was enraged. The only thing I could think of was, Why does America seem determined to murder her greatest men? Hamilton, Lincoln, Kennedy, Martin, and now Reagan too, it seemed, was to be lost when we needed them most.

Most conservatives seem to want to forget that President Kennedy accomplished three critically important missions as our nation's leader. First, he was a champion of civil rights for all Americans. John Kennedy helped us to learn that civil rights is not a racial issue, it is an American issue. Second, Kennedy revitalized the economy and initiated the longest peace-time expansions of our economy until that point in history. And, third, Kennedy's economic-tax policies were the most successful in American history. For the first time since Thomas Jefferson, Kennedy applied common sense to economic policies. The Scriptures teach us in all matters of government to give "honor where honor is due." Our nation owes a debt of gratitude and honor to John Kennedy for these three things.[1]

Likewise, President Reagan accomplished three critically important things. First, President Reagan's foreign policy was masterful. Reagan participated in the most significant and positive political changes in world history. The world changed: dramatic, turbulent, and dangerous changes. Under Reagan's leadership these changes were peaceful. Never before in history have such overwhelming political changes occurred in a time of peace! Second, Ronald Reagan revitalized the economy and initiated the longest peace-time expansions of our economy in history—longer than Kennedy's economic expansion. Hopefully, this record will be broken soon. And, third, Reagan learned his economic-tax strategy directly from the master: John Kennedy. Kennedy! No joke.

Kennedy and Reagan agreed on economic and tax strategies for the nation. Both led the nation to make the largest tax cuts in American history. Both rejected government spending merely to stimulate economic activity. The economic policy of each was a towering success. Surprised?

That's not all. No American presidents in history had an economic and tax policy more successful than John Kennedy or Ronald Reagan. These two Americans are in a class by themselves. Yes, they made mistakes too, some serious. America should celebrate and study what they did well and learn to avoid their failures.

The key to the economic successes of Kennedy and Reagan is that they rejected Keynesian economic theory as a viable tool of public policy. Both men believed Keynesian economic policy led our country into economic stagnation. They were right.

The Keynesian economic model endorses government intervention (interference) in the economy and promotes deficit spending. Both of these great men were uncomfortable with such policy directions and adopted a more conservative economic and tax policy. Reagan and John Kennedy respected Milton Friedman, a leading conservative economist, who expressed powerful new non-Keynesian economic ideas, saying, "Freedom is a rare and delicate plant. . . . History confirms, that the greatest threat to freedom is the concentration of power. . . . By concentrating power in political hands, government is . . . a threat to freedom."[2]

Milton Friedman sounds positively Jeffersonian. Friedman's ideas called for less government fiscal intervention in the economy. He believed the market economy is capable of self-regulation and the most efficient allocation of economic resources possible. Friedman believed that the scope of government in the economy should be strictly limited and focused upon actions that make the economy more free, not less. He also believed government policy decisions should be decentralized.

There have been numerous books written on the topic of misguided federal public policy. We will only touch on a very few general issues. However, the fact that we have spent in excess of $3.5 trillion in the past thirty years on entitlement programs and social policy hangs like a toxic cloud over the American economy. The damage done to the black family is immeasurable.

The Traditional Black Family

Recently, I attended a wonderful wedding for a dear friend, a black man. The wedding was a large formal dinner party complete with a band and excellent food. My wife and I had a blast.

My friend was widowed nine years ago. I love my friend dearly, but he's just a regular guy. His new wife, on the other hand, is quite extraordinary, an intelligent, beautiful lady, who was widowed five or six years ago. After her husband's death, she went back to school to earn a Ph.D. Sadly, the federal government did all it could to prevent this wedding!

This dear lady was widowed with two children to raise. The federal government provides a variety of Social Security and other benefits to support her and her children as long as they are students. These support payments continue undiminished so long as she remains unmarried. Her marital status directly controls the dollar amount of benefits to which she is entitled. Her deceased husband had a good job and paid the high Social Security taxes necessary to qualify his family for social security assistance. This assistance was not given to his family; he paid for the privilege to protect his family with social security coverage. To have this assistance denied or restricted merely due to her marital status is ridiculous!

Federal social policy should encourage the traditional middle class nuclear family model. At the very minimum, federal social policy should be neutral on the family. However, since Lyndon Johnson's 1964 administration, federal policy has been decidedly antifamily. Nearly every social program, entitlement program, or welfare program sponsored by the federal government has restrictions or benefits based upon the family's situation. If you have more babies, you get more money. If your husband abandons you, you get more money. Why would our federal government attack the traditional black family structure? It worked well before the government's intervention with liberal social policies. Our government's antifamily bias is now politically entrenched, and our society is paying the price for destroying tens of millions of black families.

Black families were traditionally nuclear, with a husband and a wife at the head of a family. This strong family unit was dedicated to the love and nurturing of the children. To suggest that the traditionally nuclear family model does not apply to the black family is, to me, a very serious form of racism. Such a suggestion implies that black men do not love their wives as much as the middle-class American norm. It also implies that black parents do not love their children as much as white people. These suggestions are worse than ridiculous; they are evil, racist ideas.

In fact, the traditional black family unit may be more rich than their white counterpart. Pre-colonial African culture extended the definition of family to include the entire clan.[3] The African proverb, "It takes an entire village to raise one child," often quoted today, indicated something of the cultural depth of the black family. Before our government's antifamily attack on the black family, there was a certain sense of community to the black family, a positive sense of clan that looked back to African roots. This concept of the community or clan as a part of the family is difficult, maybe impossible, for America's white middle class to comprehend.

The post–Civil War black family survived to become legendary for its powerful commitment to family. Alex Haley's *Roots*, especially the television version, is now a part of American culture. Haley painted a picture of the African family that suffered un-

speakable oppression but always survived because of a strong, almost mystical love. Maybe *Roots* was more fiction than genealogy;
however, it presented powerful new ideas about the black family
unit to America. My academic study of the black family and my
rereading of *Roots* both confirm this biblical model as the basis for
the traditional black family unit.

God created the family unit, black or otherwise, for the care
and nurture of the children. Love and the powerful lifetime com-
mitments of a married couple are God's unique glue to hold
families together. God's glue is powerful stuff. It is enduring.

The Destruction of the Black Family

It would take something exceedingly powerful to destroy a
social and cultural heritage as rich as the black family. In fact, it
would take the entire power of a mighty nation. In the preface to
her book, K. Sue Jewell states, "Liberal social policy, as imple-
mented in the United States, has had an adverse effect on black
two-parent families."[4]

In spite of the federal government's intense interference in the
black family and economic pressures to destroy the black family,
the black family is more healthy than most Americans realize. As
of 1988, "against extraordinary odds" approximately 55 percent of
black two-parent families remain intact.[5] But, the health of the
black family continues to decline. We need to make changes in
federal policy before we completely destroy the resiliency of the
black family. Misguided federal social policy must be changed.

There is a direct link between expensive social programs and
misguided federal tax policy. High taxes, necessary to fund liberal
social policy, have taken far too much wealth away from the
economy thereby restricting free markets. Such tax policies confis-
cate economic capital needed by the economy, reduce growth, and
limit opportunity. Instead of working to guarantee equal economic opportunity, federal tax policy makes the economy less free
for everyone.

Federal policy in support of equal access to the economy for
all Americans would be a much needed and welcome change from
our current government policy. Such policy would expand the
middle class and the amount of wealth controlled by the middle

class. Multiple millions of poor would be economically elevated into the swelling ranks of a large and stable American middle class. However, current federal economic policy seems to be one of restricting and limiting the economy thereby making more people poor. I can see no good result from policies that weaken the middle class and create more poor families. Obviously, federal reforms to expand the middle class, such as a policy of equal access to the economy, would be a welcome change.

In some cases, misguided federal tax policy actually triggers economic down-turns called recessions. The tax policies of Presidents Jimmy Carter and George Bush are perfect examples of recessions triggered by bad tax policy. Federal tax policy seems blind to any logic whatsoever.

Any CPA or tax lawyer could write a book on the topic of misguided tax policy. I will avoid the temptation and promise to limit myself to only one example of bad tax policy.

At President Clinton's urging, Congress has, for the second time, reduced the deductibility of business entertainment expenses from 80 percent to a mere 50 percent tax deductible. This is, in effect, a restrictive tax imposed upon small business. A restrictive tax means a certain activity is more expensive and therefore less likely to happen. Businessmen will simply have fewer business meals and less business travel.

You may remember that Jimmy Carter also went after this deduction with his famous slogan, "the three martini lunch," and reduced the deduction from 100 percent to 80 percent. We do not often think of Jimmy Carter as particularly gifted in economic-tax matters, yet President Clinton is taking his tax lessons from Mr. Carter's administration. I have to admit, I find it somewhat amusing that Ronald Reagan learned his approach to economic-tax matters from John Kennedy. However, Bill Clinton, a Kennedy wanna-be if ever there was one, learned fiscal policy from Jimmy Carter.

Clinton and Congress really believed they would increase revenues by six or eight billion dollars with this tax measure. Wrong! What they did was to destroy a small portion of the American tax base. The businessmen simply will eat out less often and seek alternatives to travel, such as telephone marketing.

This new law points out several problems with American tax policy. This restrictive tax on business meals is designed to reduce business activity in the restaurant and related travel industries. A decline in either business activity or capital shrinks the tax base. However, the tax expenditure analysis tools used by the administration and Congress to formulate tax policy has no concept or method for calculating the adverse effects of tax policy on business activity or capital. Such economic costs are not even considered.

Furthermore, this 50 percent tax policy limiting business meals shows a bias against small businesses owned by the middle class. Wealthy businessmen will not be deterred by this misguided tax policy. However, wealthy businesses account for only an insignificant portion of this nation's spending in the restaurant and travel industries. The vast majority of travel and entertainment spending is done by small businessmen: solid citizens of the middle class. Also, the vast majority of restaurants in America are family-owned small businesses. This law will seriously hurt their businesses as well.

And finally, this travel and entertainment policy will put tens of thousands of restaurant and travel industry employees out of work. Antiemployment legislation is not wise; our economy is still a bit fragile. Most of these displaced workers will be low-paid, entry-level employees; many will be black. We particularly do not need antiemployment legislation against people who need economic assistance the most.

This type of tax policy has a distinct Hamilton-Federalist flavor. It attacks the middle class, making small businesses less competitive and does little or nothing to equalize the advantages wealthy businesses have over small business. Tax policies that keep the rich on top and work against the middle class have been the norm of American tax policy for most of my life. There have been very few exceptions.

Carter's old slogan in support of his antimiddle class policy, "the three martini lunch," is most deceptive. It implies a policy aimed at the rich, when in reality this tax increase hurts the middle class deeply. Carter and Clinton want to dress up and masquerade as Jeffersonian when they are, in fact, elitist Hamilton-Federalists.

Under the liberal's banner of fairness, the rich get richer at the expense of the middle class. Liberal social and tax policy has taken the majority of the poor and kept them poor.

In fact, thirty years after the most important equal rights legislation in our history, the majority of black people believe they are less well-off financially. Historically, federal policies have kept poor people poor. Now it seems as if these misguided policies are pushing more people into poverty. Such policies are not in the best interest of America or the Church.

If I was paranoid, I could find a conspiracy in there somewhere. But, there is no conspiracy, just plain old fashion stupidity. We have too many Hamiltons; what America needs now is another Jefferson.

Many of our tax policies hurt small businesses far more than they hurt larger and wealthier businesses. By the smallest amount, this particular tax policy limiting the deduction for business meals, reduces free and fair markets necessary to the smooth running of our economy. This tax law, combined with all the other anti-investment, antiemployment, antismall business legislation, creates a consistent picture of federal policy as antipoor and antimiddle-class. Politicians can tell you that it's not so with political slogans and ideology, but actions and results speak louder than denial.

What would good tax policy for travel and entertainment expenses deductions be like? Deductions for everybody! I am serious; deductions for everybody: individuals, corporations, partnerships, everybody! Now that would be Jeffersonian-style taxation.

With these deductions, working moms and dads are put on a truly equal tax footing with big businesses and the superrich because they would get their tax deduction too! Eating out is no longer a special treat for a family; it has become ordinary. When mom and dad both work, it is often necessary to take the family out to eat. Most two-earner families are required by economic necessity. Our tax laws require that expenses be ordinary and necessary to justify a business deduction. Sounds reasonable to me. Having a tax deduction for merely eating out with the family is not legal under current tax policy, but it should be.

Further, the middle-class traveling salesman and small businesses would have an important economic advantage over big business. Millions upon millions of additional business lunches would stimulate sales for small businesses aggressively looking for new markets. The vast majority of this "lunch money" would be spent for benefit of small business for the simple reason that there are so many more of them.

The restaurant industry also would grow by multiple tens of billions of dollars. Millions of people would open new restaurants or find employment in the restaurant, travel, or related industries. The profits of these industries would expand by hundreds of billions of dollars.

And finally, the tax base of the nation would be dramatically improved. Federal income tax receipts, drawn from restaurants and related travel industries, would shoot up by billions of dollars. The additional revenues would more than offset the imaginary revenue lost by granting these liberal tax deductions and certainly more than the phantom revenues of misguided attempts to limit this deduction. Maybe you would need to fine-tune the tax policy a bit by putting a cap on the meals deductions of some percentage of taxable income or a flat dollar cap. Such limits may limit the loss of federal revenues and sharply tilt the tax advantage of this liberal tax policy to the middle class.[6]

Everybody wins, except possibly big business, which would lose one of many unfair competitive advantages created by misguided government tax policy. Big business and the superrich have enough money so that limitations on tax deductions will have little effect on their marketing efforts. Small businesses, on the other hand, must count every penny just to stay in business. Any antismall business tax law, like this 50 percent reduction of the tax deduction for business meals, has an immediate adverse impact on small businesses and the middle class.

Besides, what could be more fair than giving moms a tax deductible right out. She probably needs tax relief more than either the super rich or small business. If we truly want to have Jeffersonian style tax law, we must count her in.

Such a policy might even be considered profamily. Oops! I lose track of whether or not *profamily* is a politically correct term.

During the Bush-Quayle administration, *profamily* was not an acceptable political term. But, I think President Clinton has taken on Quayle's profamily mantel, so I guess the term is now correct. Political correctness gets so confusing. They should really publish dictionaries of correct terms.

What Is the Difference between Good Tax Policy and Bad?

Until very recently, the federal government was not overly concerned with economic limitations. The government was spending money like the printing presses were able to make all we ever needed. Only recently has the size of the federal debt and the obvious weaknesses in the economy due to that debt, created any legitimate efforts in the federal government to economize.

Businesses, however, must constantly economize. They exist in an environment where economic limitations can and often do put companies out of business. Business people therefore walk an economic high wire. They must spend enough money to maximize both their revenues and their bottom-line net profits.

Tax policy needs to be done in a similar manner. The federal government must seek a level of taxation that will not create a drag to limit the economy and thereby maximize the wealth of the nation. Minimal federal intervention should be limited to encouraging economic markets to become more free and open. The goal of fiscal policy should be to create a level economic playing field for rich and poor, big business and small business, black and white, in short, a level economic playing field for all Americans.

At the very least, it will require the federal government to quit playing political games of class distinction such as "the three martini lunch" or "the rich must pay their fair share" to hide the true target of tax increases. It is an indisputable economic fact that tax revenues come from the middle class. The middle class is the tax base of the nation. There is not enough wealth in the hands of the superrich, or even if the moderately rich are included, to support any reasonable tax base. Any tax increase is a middle class tax increase. Such slogans are unhealthy and fundamentally un-American. Our society must learn to limit class distinctions, not fan class prejudices in tax law or other social policy. It is inescapable that tax law and fiscal policy is also social policy; there is no distinction.

For example, our nation's recent economic experiment with the luxuries tax on cars and yachts was an effort to target a tax at the rich that backfired. The luxuries tax hit the middle class much harder than the rich. Small businesses in the business of building, transporting, and docking of yachts failed in new record numbers. Many middle class and poor people lost jobs, savings, houses, and some were even forced into bankruptcy. Car sales went down, and the auto makers in Detroit laid off hundreds of thousands of workers. Unemployment and bankruptcy are cruel taxes forced upon the middle class to pay for poor federal policy. Do not be deceived by political slogans; any tax increase is a middle class tax increase!

One complication in forming intelligent tax policy is that America's economy is surprisingly strong. Even with bad tax policy, the economy will have a natural growth. But, the level of economic growth has been sharply limited by misguided tax policy. The important question is, how much is economic growth limited by bad tax policy? Frankly no one really knows. My guess is that we have achieved less than half the growth to which the American economy is capable. If such growth were to occur and fall into the hands of an expanding middle class, all Americans would benefit. Growth, by itself is not good; growth must occur in an expanding middle class.

The goal of federal economic and tax policy for the last sixty years has been to have an economy at or near full employment without inflation. We need to experiment with a third element to federal fiscal policy: maximize the nation's wealth in an expanding middle class.

We need to experiment with tax policy. We need more data available so that the academic community can develop economic models able to accurately predict the effects of tax policy on business activity and capital. At this point, the federal government has limited data from which to make reasonable predictions of the effects of new taxes on the tax base of the nation. It takes a brave president to experiment with something so complex as tax policy—brave like Kennedy and Reagan.

Changing federal tax laws, without studying the available data in tax history, will allow policy errors to reoccur and the damage done by these errors to be amplified in the economy. Some politicians call the process tax reform; I call it stupid. We all know how Carter's tax reform worked: 21 percent interest rates and a 22 percent inflation level.

Inflation is another cruel tax to pay due to poor federal policy. Remember Jimmy Carter's 22 percent inflation rate? Cruel is an accurate description of what this level of inflation did to the poor and formerly middle-class retirees on a fixed income who unexpectedly found themselves poor. Inflation is a tax, a cruel tax! Inflation creates the temporary illusion of prosperity at the same time it undermines the economy.

Interest rates above a baseline norm of about 7 to 8 percent are also an unfair tax on businesses and consumers alike. Carter's 21 percent interest rates caused the bankruptcy of millions of America's middle class. High interest rates and bankruptcy are cruel taxes to pay for misguided federal tax policy. Carter raised taxes; Reagan and Kennedy sharply cut taxes. The empirical data indicates that tax reductions are in the best interest of the economy. Jimmy Carter either did not know his tax history or ignored John Kennedy's lessons in taxation. Some people claim that Jimmy Carter is smarter than Ronald Reagan. Yep, there's that old Hamilton-Federalist elitism creeping into the public debate again. Reagan may not be smart, but his economic polices worked!

I am an unashamed Reagan fan. He initiated a brave tax experiment, and it worked! I admit he cheated a bit. He read the tax history of the Kennedy administration. Not only did it have the right questions, it gave the answers. College was never so easy.

Reagan lowered tax rates, and federal tax revenues dramatically increased. The ranks of the middle class increased as millions of poor people rose to a new economic status. Even the rich lost a small bit of their many advantages over the middle-class business people. The percentage of income paid in taxes by the upper 5 percent of wealthy Americans actually increased over Jimmy Carter's tax levels.

Reagan's plan was excellent; Kennedy's plan was better. Both plans relied upon massive tax cuts. Kennedy's tax rate cut was 20 percent, Reagan's tax cut was 22 percent. But, Kennedy's tax cuts were actually larger than Reagan's due to the innovative way Kennedy used tax credits to focus his tax cuts in such a way as to cause maximum economic growth.

Kennedy encouraged investment in business capital by inventing the "investment tax credit," which was initially an 8 percent reduction in taxes on the cost of business equipment purchased and placed in use. This tax credit, later increased to 10 percent, was an important benefit to small businesses. It helped them to finance new equipment and made small businesses more competitive and more profitable. Higher profits expanded the tax base, and federal tax revenues increased significantly. These 1962 changes in tax law under the Kennedy administration were the most courageous experiment in federal taxation in the history of America. Before John Kennedy, massive tax reductions to stimulate the economy were never considered by the Executive Branch.

The Kennedy reductions in personal and corporate income tax rates in 1962 were an important experiment with federal tax policy. In 1962, the nation was in a deep recession. The economy had stagnated. Traditional Keynesian economics, as applied by politicians, called for increased federal spending to stimulate the economy. A tax cut was a radical departure from this tradition. At the time, some people accused Kennedy of playing politics with the economy. If he was, it worked. In American politics, results count.

The Kennedy administration decided in 1962 not to increase public spending; rather it would reduce the income taxes on individuals and corporations in order to stimulate private market demand. The administration, in their proposals to Congress, argued that decreasing income tax rates would actually increase total tax revenues by increasing business activities and profits subject to taxation. The genius of John Kennedy is that he accurately predicted the results of his tax experiment before it was law.

History supports the validity of Kennedy's tax-reduction experiment: personal income tax collections increased from $45.6 billion in 1962 to $48.6 billion in 1964, while corporate income tax collections for the same period increased from $20.5 billion to $23.5 billion. The tax cuts began the longest economic expansion in American history until Ronald Reagan broke the record. Kennedy would have been proud to see his phenomenal economic record broken; he was after all a true patriot. Likewise, Reagan will be proud to see his economic record broken, if we are so fortunate as to do it in his lifetime.

The success of Kennedy's plan was not hidden. The academic community is very aware of the Kennedy tax plan and its economic benefits to America: "Based upon the apparent success of this 1962 experiment, it seems reasonable to expect similar actions in the future whenever economic circumstances require them."[7]

With only two exceptions in American history, John Kennedy and Ronald Reagan, American tax law has become progressively more complex. Good tax law will be simplification in tax law.

The high cost of government red tape spent in efforts to fully comply with the tax law is an additional tax cost to small businesses. The cost of compliance with government regulation should be reduced.

We must work to limit the government's intervention in the economy thereby increasing freedom. This should always be the yardstick of good federal policy: increased freedom. Taking money from the economy that inhibits economic growth limits freedom. Giving unfair advantage to the superwealthy and multinational businesses at the expenses of small business, limits freedom. Limiting tax benefits, such as the mythical three martini lunch that supported reduced travel and entertainment tax deductions, is bad tax policy aimed at the middle class. Political rhetoric does not change the fact that such laws hurt the middle class far more than the rich.

Our economy is more free right now than at any other time in our history with only two exceptions, the Kennedy and Reagan administrations. But, we are far from free. We have two major obstacles to overcome before we can be a truly free economy: minimize government interference in the economy and make the economy more accessible to more people.

Good economic policy will throw open the doorways into the middle class and keep those doors open. We must guarantee equal opportunity in the economy although we cannot and must not attempt to guarantee equality of results.

We can achieve these new economic freedoms for America. As America grows more free for more people, we realize the dream that made us a nation. Jeffersonian-style fiscal policies are our only hope.

Endnotes

1. This is a short list of President Kennedy's accomplishments. He also established the nation's space program on which so much of our economic future depends and so much more that is outside the scope of this book.

2. Milton Friedman, "Capitalism and Freedom," University of Chicago Press, Chicago, 1982, 2.

3. Wade Nobles, "Africanity: Its Role in Black Families," *The Black Scholar 9* (June 1974): 10–17.

4. K. Sue Jewell, *Survival of the Black Family: The Institutional Impact of U.S. Social Policy* (New York: Praeger Publishers, 1988), ix.

5. Ibid., 103.

6. I use the term *liberal* in its true meaning. A liberal tax policy is one granting lower taxes and special deductions to help the middle class. Restrictive tax policy is one of raising taxes and taking away tax benefits from the poor and middle class. Such labels as *liberal* and its counterpart *conservative* have become so twisted that the labels are worse than useless, they've become misleading. We should avoid labels and try to deal with true meanings.

7. Ray M. Sommerfeld, Hershel M. Anderson, and Horace R. Brock. *An Introduction to Taxation* (New York: Harcourt Brace Jovanovich, 1977), 1-8.

CHAPTER NINE

Reforms:
Jeffersonian Economics

Jeffersonian economic ideas enjoyed a brief revival in the administrations of John Kennedy and Ronald Reagan—too brief and even then incomplete.

Kennedy believed that maximum economic power in the hands of the middle class would make economic markets more free and the economy more stable. Likewise, Kennedy believed that the more economic power that flows into the hands of the government's bureaucratic decision makers, the more restrictive and unstable the economy becomes. Kennedy was working hard to build a larger and more stable middle class. His economic plan worked, and for the same reasons, President Reagan's economic plan also worked well.

More economic power to the people, less to the government, is a key Jeffersonian ideal endorsed by Milton Friedman, John Kennedy, and Ronald Reagan. In the old Hamilton-Jefferson conflict between the rights of the middle-class man verses the rich aristocracy, these American presidents came down squarely on the side of the middle class. Such political conduct has an appropriate label, Jeffersonian!

In order to make the economy more free, Reagan and Kennedy put more economic power into the hands of the middle class. The largest tax cuts in history put billions of additional dollars into middle-class pockets. Private sector dollars are the most effective economic vote imaginable, the only economic vote that really counts in the long run. The direction of the economy was determined by the massive increase in middle-class economic votes. Our middle class led the nation to economic prosperity for the simple reason that it was in their best interest to do so.

The idea that these tax cuts helped the rich more than the middle class is ridiculous. The indisputable economic fact is that following these tax cuts, federal tax revenues skyrocketed as the taxable foundation of the nation expanded.[1] The business expansion of the nation was accomplished by small businesses, most of which are owned and operated by middle-class Americans. Taxes actually increased on the rich and superrich under Reagan's economic plan primarily because Reagan eliminated most tax loopholes.[2] However, Kennedy's tax plan sharply reduced taxes on the wealthiest Americans by bringing their tax bracket down a full 20 percent. In addition, Kennedy actually created a wide variety of new tax loopholes that helped the rich further reduce their taxes. Was Kennedy trying to help the rich? Not at all. Kennedy was trying to jump-start a stagnant American economy, and his plan worked! Kennedy's reasons and method for reducing taxes on the rich was pure genius.

Kennedy's tax cuts were not aimed at the rich, they were aimed at middle-class-owned small businesses. Because Kennedy wanted to help as many of these people as possible, he decided to help everybody, including the rich. However, the vast majority of the cash poured into the economy by Kennedy's tax cuts went into the hands of the middle class—not the rich. The amount of our nation's wealth controlled by the middle class overwhelms the insignificant amount of wealth in the hands of those few Americans we would call rich. Therefore, tax reductions that favor business and capital formation will disproportionately benefit the middle-class people who control most of our nation's wealth. The reverse is also true: tax policy designed to raise revenues or that inhibit the growth of capital will be paid by the middle class for the same reason. America's middle class controls the vast majority of our wealth. The American middle class is huge both in terms of numbers and wealth. A large and growing middle class makes our nation more stable. A wide divergence between rich and poor, without a middle class to buffer the extremes, causes social chaos.

There is no question that Thomas Jefferson and his disciples, like President Andrew Jackson, sought to limit the prerogatives of the American aristocracy. Odd, now America finds herself in a similar situation. Our economy is making the rich superrich and dragging the middle class into poverty. The American aristocracy is alive and doing well as we approach the twenty-first century. A study of how Jefferson faced these same problems in our history will be valuable. Although not entirely successful in eradicating these special privileges, Jeffersonian ideas and policies seriously weakened the American cult of the aristocracy. Yet, our fascination with this cult seems as if it will never end.

An Aristocracy of Robber Barons

America and the world was transformed by the Industrial Revolution. The post-Civil War period for America was one of massive industrialization, the rapid growth of cities, and the rise of the new American aristocracy, the Robber Barons.[3]

The hands-off economic policy of our government, demanded by the classical economic theory, allowed for the rise of this new American aristocracy. Names like John D. Rockefeller and Oil, Andrew Carnegie and Steel, Cornelius (Commodore) Vanderbilt and Railroads, J.P. Morgan and Banking are permanently linked in the American mind: the famous Robber Barons. These men did not amass their incredible wealth by adhering to the traditional American values of honesty, hard work, and thrift. The Robber Barons were ruthless and unscrupulous men who made their profits by using any means available to crush competitors and to corrupt politicians.

The level of political corruption during the age of the Robber Barons is hard for modern Americans to comprehend. Wholesale bribery was a routine and daily part of business life. In one bitter fight between Robber Barons that pitted Commodore Vanderbilt against Jay Gould and Jim Fisk, the fair market price of a legislator was a bribe of fifteen thousand dollars a head. One creative and influential legislator managed to collect seventy-five thousand dollars from Vanderbilt and one hundred thousand dollars from Gould. When the Commodore's lawyer advised him that certain actions he planned were illegal, he was said to thunder, "What do I care about the law? Hain't I got the power?" The Robber Barons did indeed have the power, all the political power they could buy.

Social Darwinism was Charles Darwin's theory of evolution misapplied to economic and social matters. Darwin's theory is one of history's most powerful ideas. And, like all powerful ideas, Darwinism gives people a new language to work with and a new way to consider a complex matter, the origin of various species. To most Christians, Darwin's theory has also been misapplied to Creation. In any event, Charles Darwin never intended his theory to be applied to sociology or economics. However, powerful ideas have a life of their own and live far longer than their creators.

Most of the tycoons sincerely believed they were good men who attained their wealth by exercising the old-fashioned Protestant virtues of hard work, thrift, and honesty. Never underestimate the power of the human mind to justify its own actions. To these men, they got what they deserved. Other less fortunate people were lazy or stupid. In some vague way, they believed it was all connected to the divine will of God.

Businessmen defended their actions, mouthing the clichés of classical laissez-faire economics, even though the monopolistic trusts they created were undermining even the illusion of a free competitive market and distorting, if not destroying, the foundations of supply and demand.

Herbert Spencer, an Englishman, applied Darwinism to social relationships. Spencer taught that struggle in society is normal, especially in economic life. The weak would fail; the strong will survive and become dominate. The human race would benefit because the weak were eliminated and the fit would advance the race of men as it did Darwin's animals. In hindsight, this social philosophy sounds ridiculous. It allowed justification for the rise of the Robber Barons and the destruction of the American middle class.

Being fully self-justified, the mythical laissez-faire capitalism of the Robber Barons became increasingly less free and less capable of self-regulation. As competitors were crushed by ruthless and criminal means, fewer men controlled more of America's economic resources. Between 1865, the end of the Civil War, and 1900, American businesses became less competitive. Smaller firms were merged into larger holding companies, or they were destroyed. These holding companies became gigantic monopolies called trusts. By 1900 there were more than three hundred of these trusts. In 1900, 50 percent of all the manufactured goods in the country were produced by fewer than 2 percent of the manufacturing firms. America had again become a land of a superrich aristocracy.

This level of wealth, concentrated in the hands of so few people, undermined not only the economy of America but her social and political structures as well. In the years leading up to the Great Depression, the wealth of the richest Americans rose rapidly to staggering levels while the wealth of the middle class stagnated or actually declined relative to the rich.

The abuse of labor, even child labor, was appalling. Working conditions, work hours, and poverty-level wages were the norm. The large cities, created by the Industrial Revolution, increasingly became squalid slums. The common man had little choice but to fight back; labor organized or, more correctly, tried to organize. The Robber Barons fought labor's efforts at every turn, and the fight was often brutal and tragic.

Big business could fight back with more than merely over-whelming economic power. Politicians, bought and paid for with bribes, supplied the police and the army upon request. A strike at McCormick Harvester Company (now the International Harvester Company) in Chicago became violent when police harassed the protestors. Some unknown person threw a bomb into the ranks of the police. Seven policemen were killed, and sixty-seven other people were injured. Four strikers were killed when police opened fire into the crowd. The previous day police also killed four strikers. Chicago and the business community of America were terrified, fearing an armed uprising by labor. The country panicked; many believed we were close to another civil war—this one between the aristocracy and the common man.

A few years later, two of the most violent strikes in American history occurred at the Homestead plant of Carnegie Steel Company in Pennsylvania and at the Pullam Palace Car Company in Chicago. Three guards and ten strikers were killed when a pitch battle, involving men heavily armed with guns and dynamite, ensued on 6 July 1892 at the Carnegie Steel Company.

In the Pullman Strike, over seven hundred thousand men were out on strike in 1894, a depression year. Economic conditions were so harsh that strikers were threatened with actual starvation in this depression-era strike. The company slashed wages by an average of 25 percent. Furthermore, the Pullman company owned the housing occupied by their employees but refused to proportionately reduce the rents, even though the cost of company housing was well above the local market price for comparable housing. All workers who protested the wage cuts and rental fees were discharged. The strike was eventually broken by the U.S. Army at the direction of President Cleveland and under the orders of the Robber Barons.

The age of the Robber Barons was a roller-coaster ride of boom and bust cycles: the depression of 1874 to 1880, the downturn of 1883 to 1886, the panic of 1893 to 1894, the panic of 1907, the depression of 1922 to 1923, and the Great Depression of 1929 to 1941.[4]

In my opinion, each of these depressions had the same root cause, the lack of free and economic markets. The Robber Barons, with their ruthless business practices, monopolized our economy and destroyed the free markets. Without free markets, capitalism can't self-regulate. The American economy became centralized in the hands of a small group of powerful men. But, the Robber Barons could not plan or control a centralized economy. Since the beginning of the Industrial Revolution, no one in history has been able to plan or control a centralized economy. Given the collapse of the Soviet Union, it appears that central economic control is impossible. The Soviet Union for over seventy years diligently relied upon centralized economic planning and control only to fail miserably. Without free markets, bad economic decisions were made, and the same errors are repeated and amplified.

The Robber Barons created a distorted economy where the rich got fabulously rich while the common man stagnated or grew more poor. There was little room in this distorted economy for a middle class. One of the most telling symptoms of a sick economy is the size and financial condition of the middle class. A large, stable, and affluent middle class has always been a stabilizing force in society. In America we have such a middle class, except among blacks. And, the lack of a large black middle class indicates serious social and economic problems.

The age of the Robber Barons, also called the Gilded Age, was a time of apparent prosperity. Huge investments were made in industrial capital. New industries were being created. Without economic restraints, industrial capacity was created far beyond market needs.

The 1920s was also a time of overconstruction. Business and residential construction during the post-World War I period occurred at a furious pace, making up for the lost war years. By 1926, the construction boom had leveled off and began to decline. Long before the stock market crash, the construction industry collapsed.

Huge investments in excess industrial capacity were funded, in part, by debt. Consumer debt, mortgage debt on new houses, and debt to purchase speculative stocks all mushroomed. Installment debt allowed consumers to purchase new durable goods available in the 1920s. The go-go mentality of the Roaring Twenties caused people to spend beyond their financial means. People felt the need to participate in the apparent prosperity of the times. Even though the wealth that funded the Roaring Twenties was largely restricted to the elite or superwealthy, the middle class wanted to enjoy the good life as well. The middle class did make financial gains in the 1920s; however, the superwealthy aristocracy grew richer and faster than the middle class. The division between rich and poor grew ever sharper.

The middle class seemed more interested in the appearance of prosperity than in their own underlying economic reality. Consumer debt became an acceptable way of life. Home mortgages increased rapidly, only to see the construction industry collapse and property values fall. Many people found themselves in the uncomfortable position of owing more debt on their houses than the value of their mortgaged property. Consumers began to realize that the apparent prosperity of the late 1920s was largely an illusion for them.

One of the most disturbing uses of debt was to finance speculations in stocks and bonds. This debt-financed speculation precipitated the stock market crash of October 1929.

A shrinking money supply, called deflation, and the rapid contraction of debt, along with a wide array of other factors such as a large number of weak banks and shrinking consumer markets, worked together to trigger the stock market crash. When stock values fall, the value of the stocks as collateral for debts also falls. The market's slump became a crash as speculators were required to sell devalued stock to pay off debts.

The blind optimism of the 1920s pushed stock prices to levels out of touch with market realities. The companies, represented by the stocks being traded, could not possibly earn the profits necessary to justify these inflated stock prices.

Many speculators made stock purchases with debt. When the stocks became worthless, the debts remained. The exuberant optimism of the Roaring Twenties gave way to a deep and crippling national pessimism, which made it impossible for the nation to invest in new economic capital. Without new investments, the economic downturn in the nation's economy could not be repaired. America was in a depression which seemed to have no end.

Restrictive taxes, designed to protect domestic workers from rigorous international competition, backfired. Instead of preserving jobs, these high taxes shut down international trade causing markets to shrink, amplified the unemployment crisis, and deepened the depression.

These high taxes, in restraint of free trade, only served to intensify the real problem underlying the Great Depression, the lack of free markets. Monopolies, bribery and political corruption, criminal business practices, and violence strangled the last glimmer of free and competitive markets in America. These high taxes, called tariffs, destroyed the last hope of market competition and self-regulation. With no free market competition available anywhere, the Great Depression became inevitable.

Keynesian economics was embraced by our nation's policymakers out of desperation in the dark days of the Great Depression. John Maynard Keynes, an economic genius, devised new ideas that gave nations a framework to understand and manage their economies. Prior to Keynes, this had never been done. The very idea of managing an industrial era economy was almost blasphemy.

America's leaders, in desperation, latched on to these new ideas. Keynesian ideas allowed the federal government to take economic actions with some belief that such intervention would help a desperate nation. Under Keynesian influences, the federal government would increase its net spending to stimulate economic activity and increase consumer demand. Increased demand would further stimulate the economy creating a cycle that would, theoretically, break the grip of the Great Depression and restore the economy. Deficit government spending was considered necessary and helpful in certain economic circumstances. Deficit spending is, in fact, required by the Keynesian economic model.

In an effort to break out of the Great Depression, our leadership adopted Keynesian ideas and initiated the most massive federal economic intervention until our recent history. Franklin D. Roosevelt began the alphabet soup of Keynesian-motivated spending programs, AAA, NRA, TVA, and a slew of additional programs, all aimed at deficit-spending us out of depression. American's fondly remember F.D.R. as our leader who restored hope in America's future and who led us through the two most dangerous crises in our nation's history, the Great Depression and World War II.

It is easy to see how we could forget that his economic programs failed. The New Deal failed to bring about a full recovery. World War II ultimately broke the depression, not Keynesian economics. As much as both John Kennedy and Ronald Reagan admired F.D.R., neither was blind to this fact.

Keynesian-initiated spending programs have unfortunate drawbacks. They made deficit spending politically acceptable, and our economy is now paying a high price for deficit spending. Unfortunately, many of our political leaders still believe deficit spending is acceptable.

Under Keynesian influences, the government would have to increase spending without increasing taxes in order to bring total market demand up to an acceptable level. This model fostered the belief that business and capital investment may not be very sensitive to changes in tax costs and interest rates; therefore, an over-emphasis was placed on fiscal intervention as the primary tool of federal economic policy. These shortcomings of Keynesian economics are not even the most serious.

The time lag required to determine that the economy is in trouble, to design and implement economically sound projects, and reap the hoped for economic benefits is ridiculously long. Furthermore, once an economic assistance program is in place and voters become dependent upon it for their family's welfare, it is difficult to terminate even when economic conditions change, not to mention the fact that it may be politically unwise to terminate these programs. Termination of such programs appears unfair. This is the root of the modern fairness doctrine of which you may have heard. This doctrine is used as justification for refusing to terminate unwise and unsound spending programs or for beginning new spending programs which have known adverse economic consequences.

However, the most serious failing of Keynesian economics, as applied by politicians, is that it focuses attention on the government as the central component of the economy. The impact of small businesses and investors on the economy is, to some degree, ignored. Unfortunately, ignoring small businesses and investors has been the predominate pattern of the federal fiscal policy since the New Deal. The only exceptions are the administrations of John Kennedy and Ronald Reagan. That ridiculous and dangerous thinking leads to ideas about centralized economic planning, deeper government intervention into private economic matters, and ever higher taxes.

The indisputable economic fact is that America's economy is fueled by small businesses! Because of this misapplication of Keynesian ideas, American tax and fiscal policy has a strong anti-small business and antimiddle class tradition of bias.

Even with these political failures of the Keynesian model, the contributions of John Maynard Keynes to economics is indisputable. The Keynesian model provides valid ways for economists to understand national economies. The failure of the Keynesian model is in its political applications, not its scholarship. Keynesian economics is an original set of ideas in a supremely complex field. John Keynes truly deserves the title of genius. His ideas are powerful and still widely used, or misused, today.

Keynesian ideas have blended into and become a part of every modern economic school of thought, and even outdated Keynesian ideas are still embraced by many politicians who find Keynesian economic ideas appealing because they seem to indicate that they can actively intervene in the economy and accomplish positive results. Politicians, above all else, want to be seen as actively doing something meaningful. Other economic schools of thought, which indicate that proactive political intervention is not helpful are obviously not as appealing to a politician. The issue is not the validity of the economic theory being applied, but the posturing of politicians.

Most economists and historians now agree that Keynesian political-economic ideas of the 1930s were flawed. However, the nation's need for a new way to understand economic problems during the Great Depression was overwhelming. The Great Depression was an economic catastrophe for which the American public demanded political explanations and action. The economic problems were real, that much was obvious, but, at the time, the causes of the Great Depression were much less obvious.

Prior to the Great Depression, the government took a hands-off approach to the economy in the belief that pure laissez-faire capitalism was capable of self-regulation. Called the classical theory, this political-economic belief had one overwhelming flaw. Laissez-faire capitalism depends upon pure and perfect markets. American capitalism, prior to the Great Depression, was not pure, perfect, nor free. Most poor and middle-class people were locked out of the tremendous wealth created by the pre-Great Depression economy. This economy was ruled by the infamous Robber Barons.

The government's hands-off economic policy, due in large part to a misapplication of Jeffersonian ideas, was rooted in the belief that the federal government should minimize its interference in the private economic lives of its citizens. In Jefferson's day, the economic battle was between those who controlled the factors of production and those who wanted free access to the economy. The economic struggles of today, and all through America's history, have been some variant on the same theme: the haves versus the have-nots. In America, these two classes of people have always been locked in a political-economic struggle to fairly allocate our nation's economic resources. History tells us that the entire nation gains prosperity when this struggle is decided on the basis of greater freedom for more people. Equal access to the economy is not only good politics, it is good economics.

When our nation was born, these two classes of people, the haves and the have-nots, were the larger farmers and wealthy merchants supported by Hamilton's Federalists and the small farmer and common man supported by the Jeffersonians. Jefferson saw a need for economic reform to make more equal the economic opportunity between these classes of people. On the other hand, the Federalists sought to protect the aristocracy's traditional dominance in the economy. Only the particular players in this economic clash change, the underlying themes do not. We will be having similar economic disputes in the twenty-first century, probably the twenty-second century as well.

As Thomas Jefferson pointed out in his own economic reforms, government intervention into the economy is, at times, necessary in order to make capitalism more free. American capitalism has not, nor will it ever be, pure, perfect, or completely free. It is simply impossible. To make government policy on the assumption of perfect markets is ludicrous. Such self-regulating laissez-faire capitalism requires a world full of pure and perfect people. Our government should be involved in the economy only to the minimal extent necessary to make the economy more free. Our political standard on fiscal and tax policy should always be, make America's economy more free.

Our modern economy is surprisingly healthy given the long history of government abuse heaped upon it. Our government's attempts to control the economy are too invasive. The level of wealth removed from the economy and invested in government programs is far too high. Too much economic power in the hands of too few government bureaucrats undermines free economic decision making like the Robber Barons of years gone by. The results may well be the same: a roller coaster ride of economic ups and downs with another Great Depression in our future. Our government's interference in the economy is far too large and must be limited.

Our economy, to be healthy, must be largely controlled by small businesses and the middle class. Legislation to protect and promote this class of people is good economic law. Anything else is a gross misapplication of federal power that will make the economy less free and therefore less prosperous.

Private economic trends that bring the poor up to middle-class economic status are good trends that must be encouraged. Government programs cannot accomplish this task effectively for the vast majority of poor people. In fact, most government programs will have the opposite long-term effect of keeping poor people poor. Government-provided welfare is a travesty of justice. The most tragic victims are the poor who remain trapped in a cycle of poverty.

Transferring these welfare programs from the federal government to the states will not improve the long-term negative effect of welfare. It is simply replacing one set of bureaucrats with another. There is only one legitimate solution to this particular dilemma: privatize the entire welfare system from funding to management. It can be done.

The multitrillion dollar spending on federal entitlement programs requires massive tax revenues. Support of these spending programs has forced our government to take far more taxes out of our economy than is economically wise. Entitlement programs as of 1993 amounted to $738 billion each year, nearly half of our $1.497 trillion federal budget. The American economy is capable of taking a major portion of the money now being spent in entitlement programs as investment capital, creating huge amounts of wealth for all Americans. Such economic policy would expand the ranks of the middle class as America's poor become poor no more.

Endnotes

1. This is called the tax base in the popular tax expenditure analysis taxation model.

2. Reagan's decision to eliminate most of the available tax planning opportunities, i.e., loopholes, was, in my opinion, a mistake and the

only weakness in his tax policies. John Kennedy did not make this same mistake.

3. The term *Robber Barons* was coined by Matthew Josephson in his book *The Robber Barons* (New York: Harcourt, Brace and Company, 1934).

4. The panic of 1907 caused the federal government to turn to one of the Robber Barons, J.P. Morgan, to save the nation from financial collapse. Mr. Morgan was the only person rich enough and with prestige enough to pull the bank together and weather the panic of 1907.

CHAPTER TEN

Reforms:
Politically Active Christians

We are unique among nations. Our American Revolution was not merely against England but against an eighteenth-century world where the rights of aristocracy were assumed to be God-given. Today, we assume the rights of the new American aristocracy to be political business as usual in Washington. As a nation we have made a lot of mistakes. The American cult of the aristocracy may be our greatest error.

We forget just how young America is when we fail to understand how our forefathers could make such errors in our experiment with freedom as slavery, the Robber Barons, federalism, and so many others. But, America, because of our foundation in freedom and our Constitution, can overcome such gross errors.

Liberty is not a static condition. Freedoms must continue to grow, or they will decline and die. The freedoms of speech, religion, and assembly help keep us free and, hopefully, will always make us more free. All Americans can and should participate in the process of continually making America more free. We have economic political restrictions on our freedom when our government interferes where it does not belong. These problems of government interference are easily solved at the ballot box.

Our greatest threats to freedoms, however, are not so easily solved by a ballot-box revolution. The problems of racism, lack of free access to the economy for all people, the failure of education, the rise of violence, immorality, and greed will demand different solutions, nongovernment solutions. I believe we are up to these challenges. I believe America is capable of dealing with these threats to our liberty. The Church can be a source of invaluable leadership in eliminating these threats to America's liberty—or we can become an even bigger stumbling block. The role of the Church in plotting the future of America cannot be underestimated. Whether or not this role will be for good or ill has yet to be determined.

In spite of America's shortcomings and our enormous problems, I believe America will heal. It may be a difficult and painful healing, but a bright future awaits all of us who are proud to be Americans.

One reason I am so optimistic is that the Church will get another opportunity to do as we should. We have failed on the issues of racism twice by my count; we will not fail again. I know the Church will have a third chance, one more opportunity to do this good that God intended for us. It is inevitable.

Obviously, the social programs designed to help poor Americans, mostly black people, have failed. It is also obvious that our country has drained its economy to pay for these programs. The federal government can no longer afford to pay the high price. The government must either sharply reduce these program costs to avoid national bankruptcy, or the nation will simply collapse under a mountain of debt. Either way, the social opportunities for the Church will be immediate and overwhelming. The Church must again become the primary provider of social welfare in America.

We can thank our God of second chances for this opportunity to do good. God is a God of second, third, and more chances. He will even give us seventy times seventy chances to repent and do His will. However, it has been my experience that one should obey God as soon as His will is known. Repeated repentance and re-experiencing God's grace in forgiveness is quite painful. Sin is never without consequences. True repentance requires humility before God. If necessary, God can humble America before Him. If He does so, the American Church will be humbled along with our nation. Christians will be in no position to gloat if our nation falls under the judgment of an angry God.

If our political leadership is smart (a big if!) they will opt for a controlled but sharp reduction in social spending. At the same time, making changes in tax law and economic policy to encourage the tithe, and other forms of charitable giving, and to rapidly expand the economy. The economy must grow to absorb millions of poor people who must move up the economic ladder into the middle class. These will be the newly freed economic slaves of failed federal social programs, not unlike the newly freed slaves of an earlier era of America's history. Slavery, by whatever description, is an ugly thing. The only good that can come to slavery is freedom.

The social programs we need to eliminate will be the same programs that have trapped the black community into multigenerational cycles of poverty and destroyed the traditional black family unit. These people will be frightened, angry, and unlikely to trust the Church, the government, or anybody else. We must earn their respect and trust. The Church will be a primary economic safety net as the government-provided safety net unravels. We cannot fail them again. The Church cannot abandon people. After two hundred years of God's chastisements on the issues of racism and materialism, I hope we have learned our lessons. We cannot and must not fail again. Either we bring freedom to Americans locked in poverty, or we will bring slavery down on all of us.

The other alternative is more bleak. However, the results will be the same. The Church cannot and, I believe, will not fail again. We will become the primary provider of social welfare to America's poor.

If our political leadership is unwise (a distinct possibility), the government will allow itself to collapse under a mountain of debt, the economy will be in shambles, and America will be gripped by a deep national pessimism. Social problems will be out of control. Starvation may be a real possibility for many people. The American Church has been in precisely this same situation on two prior occasions and failed.

We failed once after the Civil War when the nation was in the grip of a massive postwar depression. The Church was called on to care for the newly freed blacks and others left destitute and broken by war. Our clear call, directly from God as revealed in Scriptures, was to a ministry of healing to a broken land. The

Church refused to help! We openly denied God, and America has paid the price.

The second failure of the American Church was in the Great Depression. The social needs of the poor, both black and white, were overwhelming. In both of these cases, the Church was broken and hurting, like the entire nation. We had no money and little hope. These were our excuses for abandoning the Word of God and the teachings of our Lord. We even forgot how to love.

If and when a collapse of social spending comes, America and the Church may find themselves in a situation similar to these historical parallels. The Church may again be pessimistic, desperately poor, and facing social problems beyond our comprehension. The Church may have little to share, but we will have God's love and abundance to call upon. We will also have these prior historic experiences from which to learn. We have been through this situation twice before; this time we cannot forget how to love with God's action-oriented agape love. The Church will not fail again! It is for this very reason that God has blessed us with His spirit of renewal in the American Church. God is preparing us for our time of opportunity.

I am not optimistic without good cause. I believe in God. I believe the modern outpouring of God's spirit upon the Church is to will and work for His good pleasure. It is the pleasure of God for the Church to come to the aid of people in times of need. I believe in the Word of God and the power of prayer. And, I believe in the Church, the bride of Jesus Christ. God will not do our work for us; He has made that clear. However, if we are committed to a godly purpose as the Church, God will support our mission and nothing can block our success (Rom. 8:31).

The issues we face are real. The solutions will not be simple. The price of our failure may well be another Great Depression, deeper than the first or, God forbid, another Civil War. We are in a political-economic situation with extremely high stakes and great risks. The Church cannot, must not, and will not fail in our responsibilities again! Our nation will not tolerate another failure of the Church in her hours of deepest need. I shudder to think of God's judgment on the Church in the event of another failure.

The surface issues we face are obvious: poverty, violence, failure of education, racial problems, and declining morality. There are other related problems such as drugs, gangs, and property crimes of all sorts. These are the results of sin in our society and sin in the Church (Rom. 6:23). Those who abandon God says Hosea, "shall reap the whirlwind" (Hos. 8:7). America is abandoning God; the results are unmistakable. But, these are merely surface issues; the real problems go much deeper.

When America begins to abandon God, she also begins to abandon God's ideal of freedom in favor of the enemy's doctrine of slavery. Let us never delude ourselves into thinking that slavery is dead. Slavery is alive and well and growing stronger every day in America. Poverty is slavery, so is ignorance and greed. Ask any family who has a child addicted to drugs about slavery. America is being made a nation of slaves. The absence of hope is, by definition, slavery. A distorted economy that makes the rich superrich and squeezes the life out of the middle class is a destroyer of hope. Such an economy makes slaves of us all in one way or another.

A mission of the Church must be to break the back of slavery in America. Let us work to that end. Let's make equal access to the economy a reality. Let's rebuild excellence in education. We can restore family values and train our young in the Judeo-Christian work ethic. We can reverse the decline in morality caused by the way we abandoned the godly and ethical traditions on which America was founded.

The American Church needs a new ethical foundation to take us into the future. Our historic ethics as American Christians are seriously flawed. Our nation has no confidence that we can fulfill any mission given to us either by law in our Constitution or in faith, as revealed by the Word of God. We have made serious mistakes. It is time to repent. It is time to rediscover the ethical foundations of the kingdom of God.

We need a new ethical foundation, based upon the teachings of Christ who compels us to bring hope to the hopeless and freedom to those in bondage. Our definitions of hope and freedom need to be as big as God's meanings for these holy words. Freedom for some and not for all, is not godly freedom—it is the merest illusion of freedom for the few. Even the privileged few suffer the indignity of slavery in a nation where freedom is an illusion. These few have their own slavery in fear, greed, and, occasionally, in tragedy.

Please feel free to explore and criticize my conclusions and political agenda. I take full responsibility for them. They did not come from God, and they are certainly open to debate. Let me be perfectly clear; my ideas are just that, my own. My conclusions are not gospel, nor are they holy. These ideas are merely my way of working to free all men still held captive as slaves in America.

In fact, that is exactly what I want, criticisms and debate by Christians well-grounded in the ethical teachings of Christ. Without such open debate, Christians can never become full or legitimate partners in the political process.

But, since this is my book and I have the floor, let me tell you about my political agenda: I believe that the smaller the government, the more freedom we have for everyone. Big government means less freedom—small government means more freedom. Jefferson would have loved that statement.

One basic principal I hold to is this, the government cannot make men free. It can participate. It can help. Slavery and freedom are social issues. Only society, i.e., the private sector, can effectively deal with social issues. Social healing does not come from Washington; it comes from Nebraska, Mississippi, and grass-root Americans. Hopefully, healing can also come from Christian citizens who are committed to the godly ethics of hope and freedom for all Americans. Our most needed reforms are economic and tax reforms.

Taxes are too high. They take money away from the middle class and deprive the economy of capital. High tax rates and a slow (or no growth) economy are directly related. For example, the Institute for Research on the Economics of Taxation has determined that a 1 percent increase in payroll taxes will cause the economy to lose five hundred thousand jobs.

I like President Kennedy's approach to lowering taxes. His tax policies were precisely aimed at encouraging capital formation and building an expanding economy. We need tax reform that will lower taxes and rebuild capital. Any tax reform should bring back the Kennedy administration's investment tax credit, one of the few strokes of pure genius in the history of federal tax policy. It worked so bring it back!

Part of the problem with our tax policies is the tax expenditure analysis method Congress and the administration use to formulate tax policy. This method does not calculate the positive economic impact of lower taxes or tax deductions into tax policy decisions. The nation's tax base is treated as if it is a zero sum game. The assumptions implied by federal tax policy are that wealth in America is finite and that economic growth is divorced from tax policy. This is the classic political misinterpretation of Keynesian economics—a style of political economics rejected by Kennedy and Reagan.

Tax expenditure analysis causes the costs of tax reductions or tax deductions to be overstated, making tax reductions appear more expensive in terms of lost federal tax revenues than they would actually be. Misapplied and misunderstood economics in politics have had dire adverse consequences on America.

There is more than enough data and research available to prove the flaws in the tax expenditure analysis approach. Yet, Congress is slow to abandon the traditional methods they have used for the last twenty or so years. Tax expenditure analysis is a political tool developed and adopted by so-called liberals in an effort to support their preconceived big government tax philosophy. It is almost like they are unconscious of the link between economic disaster and congressional tax policy. Voters should enlighten them!

Congress must abandon the failed tax expenditure analysis approach. In addition, we must stop punitive taxation. Punitive taxation, as you may recall, is a tax on a particular economic transaction. Prime examples are the 80 percent, now 50 percent, deductions for business meals and the luxury tax that so badly backfired. Tax law is filled with these taxes designed to limit economic activity. That's dumb! These taxes should be removed.

In fact I would go to the other extreme. If the wealthy or big business interest have a tax benefit, I would try and give the same or similar benefit to the small businesses and the middle class. For example, I would make personal restaurant bills for the middle class tax deductible. I have already explained why. The federal revenues could be protected by putting a percentage limitation on the deduction, for example, 10 percent of taxable income. Tax reform should encourage small business and the middle class. Most restaurants are small businesses.

Earl Graves, a well known and successful black entrepreneur said, "Capitalism without the capital is just an ism." Education, opportunity, and money are the three keys to unlocking the power of capitalism for Americans. Yet, our tax laws seem designed to tax and, therefore, inhibit capital formation.

Our current tax policy encourages short-term business planning and overreliance on business debt. People invest in businesses to make a profit and draw a dividend, yet we tax every dollar of dividends twice! Once as profit on the corporation level and again at the recipient level as income. Paying tax twice on the same dollar does not encourage capital.

We need several other changes in tax law. We need to change the way we tax capital gains. I would give a huge capital gains deduction of 90 percent or more, indexed, but I would want a long holding period of at least ten years. The low tax is to increase capital formation, the long holding period would encourage long-term business planning. American business planning is too focused on the next quarter and uninterested in long-term trends.

We need a variety of other changes in tax law to encourage savings such as universal IRAs and other middle-class, family-oriented programs. Tax policies allowing unrestricted ordinary income deduction for any capital lost in business start-up ventures, and unrestricted pass-through of initial start-up losses to investors, would also enhance capital formation.

Once we have a simplified tax law that encourages capital formation, laws to encourage the movement of capital into a needed direction become easier to draft. Like President Kennedy's investment tax credit, we can have minority capital formation credits, freeing capital from universal IRAs and other middle-class sources to the black entrepreneur. In fact, I have what I believe to be an excellent program worked out that will link education, opportunity, and capital to certain, high-quality minority entrepreneurs.

We have over ten thousand pages of IRS regulations alone. Add to the law itself the IRS's Revenue Rulings, IRS Procedures, and case law, and the tax law is over a half a million pages. That's too much law.

Every time a tax law is passed, it costs the government and the taxpayer time, the expense of lawyers and CPAs to understand and comply, and the cost of the tax itself. Enforcing tax law and complying with tax law is expensive. Simplifying the tax law is a good idea, but, so far, no one has ever done it.

We need to simplify the tax law. I have a plan worked out (actually I have a few economic and tax plans worked out) that will radically simplify the tax law. I call it the Triple Tithe Tax. This tax relies upon John Kennedy's idea of using tax credits to focus the economic impact of tax law.

The tax is a flat 30 percent tax, but a 10 percent credit is allowed for all charitable and philanthropic giving, and another 10 percent credit is allowed as federal education vouchers (good only in states who follow the federal program guidelines). A 10 percent flat tax remains to finance the federal government. This is a brilliant idea; I wish it was mine. Every other year or so, a 10 percent flat tax is proposed as a bill in Congress. Congress rejects the idea as simplistic. What's wrong with simple?

A 10 percent flat tax is enough revenue to fund the federal government only if welfare and many entitlement program payments are phased out and eliminated. Reduction and eventual elimination of these federal programs is in the best interest of the country, including our black citizens.

The credit for all charitable and philanthropic giving is designed to encourage people to do what is right, to give generously to people's needs. To encourage people to do what is good and right is a legitimate function of government. Government cannot do good; however, it can encourage the doing of good.

This credit will flood cash into the private philanthropic sector of our economy and allow us to achieve a key goal necessary to surviving the rocky economic road ahead of America. I believe the welfare system of the nation must be privatized. Welfare is a fact of life for two reasons: America will always have poor people who live in need, and Americans, once they are made aware of the needs of poverty, will not allow people to go hungry. Americans have the strong philanthropic instincts of a good and noble people. These healthy instincts have been blunted by decades of government policies that insulate Americans from feelings of responsibility for the welfare needs of our poorest citizens. A wall of bureaucrats and high taxes have insulated us from the true needs of the poor, making most of us believe that these are political problems belonging to the government. Privatizing welfare is not merely a solution to one of our most dangerous economic problems, it is a needed cure to restore the blunted soul of a noble people. Good medicine for the economy and good medicine for the people, sounds like good government policy to me.

Let's not deceive ourselves; this is not a perfect solution. In fact, it is a solution fraught with grave risk. As I mentioned in the beginning of this chapter, such a huge overhaul of thirty years of government policy will terrify the people most affected, the poor. They have very little reasons to trust us. This is by no means the only problem.

Obviously this 10 percent credit, or tithe, is not limited to the Church. Given the bad PR we have created, the Church will probably not be the primary recipient of this money freed from captivity in the federal coffers. The Church needs to prepare itself; the Gay and Lesbian Union and the witches and warlocks will get a share of this credit money!

As much as we may not like what they stand for, in a free society they are as entitled to receive freely given donations as we are. Our disagreements with these people do not need to be fought in Congress by legislative restrictions on them or in the courts. We need to wage our battles by redefining generally acceptable social standards. Moral leadership is a valid mission of the Church.

There does need to be some restrictions on who gets this money, but very broad restrictions designed to give people ample information to make valid capitalistic choices in their philanthropic giving. People who wish to receive money subject to the 10 percent credit need to have an annual audit on file with the local newspapers and libraries and available to any donor who asks to review a copy. The expenses reviewing audit documents, such as copies, etc., need to be paid by the interested citizen to avoid abuse. A one-page summary of the audit should be filed with the IRS and provided to each contributor with an annual statement of their contributions. Sensitive items such as compensation, fundraising and program costs, and a statement of the nature and extent of charitable and philanthropic activities must be a part of the audit and the one-page summary. That is adequate information allowing informed giving. Such a statement should replace the annual IRS Form 990 tax return for charitable organizations. The Form 990 is too complex. We must simplify tax law at every opportunity!

This will create substantial cash flow into the philanthropic community. Agencies like the Red Cross and Salvation Army, who can make productive use of the money, will get a big boost, but so will Planned Parenthood with their more liberal proabortion agenda. Many agencies that are a part of the Church will also get a fair share of this cash.

One of the functions of government is to encourage citizens to do what is right and good for the country. Encouraging citizens to support the private charitable community is good and can sharply reduce the welfare and other social burdens of government. A president using the "bully pulpit" could praise charitable hospitals and medical clinics, and the medical burdens of the poor and uninsured would be proportionately reduced.

The watch-dog press, with responsible and accurate reporting, could uncover the charlatans and the abuse, shutting off the flow of funds. The press would again be the fourth estate of government, shaping our nation with the free flow of accurate, unbiased reporting. The press has no obligation to be unbiased in their editorials. Editorials, done well, could be an important part of correcting social problems. However, unfair and biased reporting has already cost the press much credibility.

The need for education reform is discussed above; however, the funding for education reform is another, more complex, matter. The vast majority of education spending comes from state and local levels. Education is not primarily a federal spending program. However, with well-drafted legislation, the federal government can encourage the states to adopt a new funding mechanism.

A refundable credit of 10 percent of taxable income with a substantial floor to protect the poor citizens should be a credit against federal income taxes. This credit, limited to 10 percent of taxable income, will not be enough money to fund the "freedom of choice in education" and cradle-to-grave education policies I envision as necessary to social and economic reform. However, by allowing the program to be effective in only those states which approve state and local companion legislation, full funding is certain. The political pressure on states to approve these education policies will be intense.

This sort of linking federal legislation with companion state legislation is typical of the way the federal government deals with states. The most pointed example would be the release of federal highway money only to states that adopt companion legislation on speed limits, road construction, maintenance, etc. A little federal arm twisting is just political business as usual. Once again, encouraging people to do what is right is a legitimate function of government. Nothing is wrong with political arm twisting so long as arms are being twisted in the right direction.

In Alabama we are in the middle of an equity in school-funding lawsuit similar to the suits in many other states. The suit contends that school-funding per student is less among poor people and in rural areas. It is a fact that the tax base in poor and rural communities is weak; therefore, spending per student is below the average of more wealthy communities. This is a valid concern neatly addressed by a national education policy of freedom of choice in education and cradle-to-grave education. Equal funding in education would be on a child-by-child basis. If we adopt these policy positions, blacks and other minority voters will flock to the conservative political banner.

In the end everybody wins. Capitalism in the private philanthropic sector will use this tax-tithe money more efficiently. The people who need assistance will get better service, neighbor to neighbor, as it should be. Most people working in the charitable services industry are dedicated, mission-oriented professionals committed to helping people. Recipients of service will get better, get well, and come out of poverty; in general, private sector assistance is healthier for everybody. The responsibilities and burdens of government are reduced. Welfare and transfer payments are a ticking bomb politicians would like not to have sitting under their elected seats. Private-sector assistance is a politically correct way out of this dangerous maze.

The need for education reform and equal access to educational opportunities is apparent. Decentralizing education decision making by giving parents real economic power in education policy decisions will make education better. Most parents want what is good for their children and will fight to get it, if they have any hope of success. Parents give up only when they believe they have no hope of helping their children. Applying capitalistic pressures to the education monopoly will improve the quality of education. Encouraging people to have hope for their children is a valid function of government.

When presented with my ideas, some liberals have told me that parents do not care about their children. What a racist statement! Most, the vast majority, of parents love and care for their children because that is the way God made us. Parents will love their children if they are given even a hint of hope. Without hope, even something as genetically intense as parental love can die.

We already know that taxing an activity inhibits that activity. We also know, thanks to John Kennedy, that a credit or other reduction in a tax encourages the activity giving rise to a tax benefit. Why not apply this thinking to other problems like the environment?

The bottles, boxes, wrappers, and bags used in retail industries are environmentally unfriendly if for no other reason than they clog the landfills. Let's put a tax on packaging and shopping bags! Just high enough to make it sting a bit, but let's make it so no one will have to pay the tax if they recycle. That's not a bad idea. It may be the only way to kick-start the badly needed curb-side recycling industry.

Tax-environmentally unfriendly activities and give tax credits for appropriate behavior. The idea of using the tax code to inhibit unwise or unhealthy economic behavior, or to encourage other economic conduct, could make for a wide variety of interesting tax reforms. Thoughtful tax reform opens up a variety of new opportunities. We need thoughtful tax and economic reforms.

CHAPTER ELEVEN

Economic Reforms

I need to warn you: when I talk about economic reforms, I am going to knock around Wal-Mart some. But, Wal-Mart will be generic for many other companies and economic practices with which I strongly disagree.

My ideas for economic reform stand on three legs: economically friendly tax reform, equal access to the economy for all Americans (especially blacks), and support for small business. Wal-Mart and big business interests like it represents much that I find wrong with the American economy.

Let me give you a pattern. Wal-Mart comes into a community and underprices the competition. These low prices are often lower than local small businesses who can buy the same products at wholesale because big businesses can bypass the normal wholesale distribution system.

Everything is sold in this low-price economic environment: shoes, clothing, electronics, musical recordings, books, even groceries. Soon, within a year or so, small businesses in the local communities begin to shut down. Their owners are financially devastated. Then, after the competition is gone, Wal-Mart's prices begin to creep back up to near the same level of the now-failed small business units. Sometimes, Wal-Mart will actually go above the price economy of the destroyed family businesses creating a new, high-price economic environment. I call this reprehensible behavior, predatory pricing.

Riding through rural America is like turning the clock back to the Great Depression. Stores are closed and boarded up. The tax base has shrunk, so streets are in poor repair and local schools are out of money. The only oasis in these economically starved communities is Wal-Mart—bright, shiny, and new, sitting on a small rise with six acres of parking. The very people who caused the economic crisis are the only people to profit by it—Robber Barons indeed!

There is something fundamentally unfair about this scenario. It's not just Wal-Mart and small towns. This pattern is being repeated in medium and larger communities. All across America, small business is an endangered entity, driven out of existence by unfair pricing and other restrictions that deny small businesses equal access to the economy.

I know firsthand of many small businesses that have declined and some that have failed due to unfair competition. A family radio and TV store found itself selling exactly the same radios and TVs as the local K-Mart, only K-Mart retail prices were below their wholesale costs. I know of shoe stores that can't compete on price with the big chains and department stores and therefore suffered shrinking sales. Eventually, these small businesses must close their doors. Locally owned office supply stores will become a thing of the past, their owners financially devastated. Former middle-class families now find themselves struggling to maintain a middle-class lifestyle.

The Robber Baron mentality is alive and well in America: crush all competition and allow no competitor to survive. These Robber Baron business practices and equal access to the economy are at odds with one another. If our economy is to remain stable and growing, the Robber Barons' special advantages must be eliminated.

The Robber Barons of history manipulated government and politicians in order to maintain their unfair and monopolistic practices. Likewise, our new Wal-Mart-type Barons still rely on politicians to make laws favoring their business practices—not just tax laws either!

Big businesses systematically underfund retirement benefits and health care costs. Big business, in the tradition of the Robber Barons, then turns to the government for a bail-out. This pension fund bailout will cost the American taxpayers well over a $38 billion of taxpayer's money we do not have. The federal government agency, Pension Benefit Guaranty Corporation, insures retirement benefits and pension plans, sort of like the FDIC insures banks. The Department of Labor will admit to a $38 billion dollar liability, but the federal government's cost estimates are generally half the actual cost. My own estimate is far more than double the official government estimate. In my opinion, American taxpayers are facing an $80 to $100 billion bailout of big businesses due to underfunded pension liabilities. The vast majority of that money will come from the middle-class taxpayer, the home of small businesses. Small businesses will be required by law to bailout big businesses: I find the twisted road of modern Robber Baron politics bizarre at best, unfair for certain.

The underfunded health care cost liabilities of big business many well be over a trillion dollars; whatever the amount, you can bet it is a truly staggering total. Big businesses have promised their workers that they will pay for the health insurance costs of retirees. Now, big business wants to renege on this promise. For this reason, many big businesses support the new multitrillion dollar health care reforms. What a bailout! Who is going to foot the bill? It will be the middle-class taxpayer and small businesses. Twisted may be a good way to describe modern Robber Baron politics.

GM's fiscal 1993 $23 billion loss was mostly due to unfunded health care costs. Big business needs a political solution to cover their assets, shielding them from paying for these health care costs. However, when a small business incurs liability for health care or any thing else, politicians do not offer to bail them out of trouble. The middle class and small businesses will be required to pay the tax cost of this big business health care bailout.

The Robber Barons of history manipulated politicians to gain unfair advantage. Today, big business manipulates politicians to gain unfair advantage. I can see no difference. The label of "Robber Barons" may be uncomfortable, but it is accurate.

In fact, this modern pattern sounds so much like the patterns used by the Robber Barons of old it makes me nervous. The Robber Barons of the Gilded Age depended upon volume discounts in purchasing goods and transportation services to create the economic edge that kept them in power. They used predatory pricing to drive out competition. They were ruthless, not caring whom they hurt. When possible, they manipulated our government to maintain their power.

The price of the reign of the Robber Barons was the Great Depression. What will be the price America will have to pay for the new Barons of industry? Will it be national bankruptcy or a depression greater than any the world has ever seen? I can name several people, more informed than I, who believe such a tragedy is inevitable.[1] These are men I respect and admire; however, I think (or hope) they are wrong. With timely economic reform, America can escape this disaster. If such a tragedy comes, it will be the failure of our economy to allow for equal access that will be the trigger to economic disaster. Allowing modern Robber Barons special privilege is not in the best interest of America.

Avoiding economic disaster is a reasonable function of government. We should eliminate the special privilege of the "gilded few," the modern Robber Barons.

The Robber Barons of history made the economy less free and thereby triggered the Great Depression. We passed laws to protect America from these ruthless men and to cure other problems associated with the Great Depression. These were good laws that made the economy more free. Government interventions that encourage fairness and equal access in the economy are good laws. I call such good laws Jeffersonian.

The Sherman Antitrust Act of 1890 was designed to break up the monopolistic business practices that strangled free markets and choked the economy. The act was not very effective until after the Great Depression due to the Supreme Court's reluctance to enforce the law. During the Great Depression, however, it was given teeth and was used to break up powerful monopolies such as Standard Oil. The Sherman Antitrust Act is still law, although it is still not as effective as it should be. It is a good law that needs to be made better by giving it new teeth.

I like the Sherman Antitrust Act because it is the kind of Jeffersonian economic intervention we need. For the same reason, I like the Truth in Securities Act of 1933, which established the Securities and Exchange Commission. The misuse of debt in margin trading was regulated, and the act has substantially improved financial disclosures, which allow people to make more informed investment decisions. That's good law. Notice the government did not make financial decisions on behalf of the people, nor did the government insure or guarantee against loss. That sort of intervention would have been disastrous, not Jeffersonian at all. Encouraging full and truthful disclosure in business practices is good policy.

Many "Jeffersonian" economic laws were created in response to the Robber Barons and the Great Depression these Barons caused. The last I will mention is the Glass-Steagall Act, an anti-speculation law that prevented banks from engaging in high-risk securities speculation—a good law that was overturned when Congress deregulated banks and savings and loans. Banks, without regulatory restraints, reverted to pre-Great Depression investment habits. Given opportunity, any business will revert to a Robber Baron mentality, even banks. Capitalism does have problems when faced with unrestrained greed. Preventing banks and insurance companies from falling victim to their own unrestrained greed is good federal policy. Lord knows bankers need all the help they can get with the "greed" part of human nature.

The banks and savings and loans are typical; when the wealthy or big business are in a financial bind, they call upon the government for a bailout. Bailing out the banks and savings and loans will cost the middle-class taxpayers untotalled billions of dollars. As William Proxmier once noted, "A billion here and billion there and pretty soon you're talking about real money."

We need more Jeffersonian-style economic law, law aimed at removing the unfair economic advantages of the wealthy and big business. In general, we need to take some old ideas and make them better.

The Sherman Antitrust Act was designed by Congress to stop price fixing and to break up monopolies. It is a good law, but the Sherman Antitrust Act has never been as effective as it should be. We need to take this good law and make it better by making the law simpler.

These antitrust cases are complex, expensive to litigate, and difficult for jurors and judges to understand. Let's make the law simpler to prosecute and less expensive for the plaintiff. If a small business makes an antitrust claim, the big business defense lawyers will bury the injured party in huge unnecessary litigation costs such as depositions and unlimited discovery designed to discourage small town lawyers and small businesses from even raising these anti-trust claims.

Rich man's justice is a relative thing. The defendant big business in an antitrust case will have a large defense team, often a dozen lawyers or more. The local small business will have his family lawyer. The big business defense strategy is to price the local lawyer and the small business out of going to court. The rules allow for almost unlimited discovery and depositions, all very expensive costs. With good law, we should be able to make these costs more affordable or change who is responsible for paying these costs in the litigation process.

To me, there is no question that price-fixing and monopolistic business practices are bad and need to be stopped. Good law will make it easier to prove and correct. Score a big point for small businesses.

Price-fixing directly affects me. I have a medical condition known as hypertension for which I take about one hundred dollars' worth of medication each month. I have a friend who lives on the Mexican border with the same condition and medication, but he only takes seven dollars' worth of medication each month. Once each month, he steps across the border into Mexico and buys the identical medication I use from a reputable Mexican pharmacist for seven dollars. It's perfectly legal, but it is not fair. Everybody should pay the same price for the same thing. Fairness in the economy is a good thing to be encouraged.

We accuse the Japanese of unfair pricing, but they are only doing the same thing American pharmaceutical manufacturers are doing to me. It's not right when the Japanese dump products on the American economy at prices below their domestic market. It's also not right when American companies do the same things. I do not like unfair pricing when the Japanese are guilty. I like it less when Americans are equally guilty and pointing fingers of blame at the other guy. This stuff ought to stop! Special pricing, depending upon whether the product is for an export or domestic market, is wrong. Prices should be the same for all customers. Anything less is price-fixing and should be illegal.

For the same reasons, I do not like volume discounts. Volume discounts are a form of price-fixing. These discounts are the same monopolistic practices the Robber Barons used to create unfair competitive advantages. The new Wal-Mart-type business Barons of our modern economy are relying on this unfair price-fixing advantage. Volume discounts should be illegal.

I believe we should modify the Sherman Antitrust Act price-fixing provisions to outlaw all forms of price-fixing including volume discounts. When a shoe manufacturer sells a pair of shoes to a retailer, it should be the same price to Wal-Mart or the locally owned shoe store. The same should be the policy for all products, electronics, groceries, everything. We should eradicate all forms of price-fixing from our economy. Equal access to the economy is fair! And, to encourage equal assess to the economy is a legitimate function of government. A free economy is more efficient and more humane than an economy dominated by big business and their monopolistic practices.

This would not shut down the big retailers—pricing is not their only competitive advantage—but it would be a major boost to small business to eliminate the immoral price-fixing we now have in our economy. Boosting small business is important to America; it stabilizes the economy and allows for the expansion of and new entries into the middle class. An expanding middle class is the only hope of breaking the back of poverty in America.

By removing immoral price-fixing, a start-up business will have one less disadvantage to forfeit to his more well-established rivals. With price advantages eliminated, service again becomes important. In the long run, consumers will win. The upward price adjustments implied by such a policy are modest. Wait until you hear the hue and cry of big business! They'll claim inflation rates of 25 percent, massive unemployment, etc. Don't listen to them; they fear honest competition. Listen to small business people and their organizations.

Furthermore, I believe that an American economy, built on small business and the middle class, is healthier than the Wal-Mart-type economy we now have. I also believe that tax law should always encourage sound economic behavior. With rare exceptions, punitive taxation always hurts small business more than big business. We do not have to punish anyone with tax laws. Rather, tax laws that encourage good behavior are good laws.

A tax law to help small business may be a refundable credit against payroll taxes. Payroll taxes is a harsh reality for anyone starting a small business on a shoestring budget. Payroll taxes on compensation can quickly reach 10 percent of wages, or higher, depending upon local taxes. A small business on a shoestring budget can easily spend this tax money before the various government taxes are paid. Getting behind in payroll taxes, in my experience, is the most common direct cause of business failure.

We could help these shoestring businesses get going with a very simple credit: reducing payroll taxes. The credit could be refundable—a welcome rebate from the government to help finance a business start-up. For example, a credit of 5 percent of all compensation paid that decreases to 4 percent when profits top one hundred thousand dollars and continues to phase out at the rate of 1 percent for every one hundred thousand dollars in taxable income. What a shot in the economic arm! Even better, it wouldn't cost the government a cent in lost revenues. Revenues would actually increase with increased economic activity. Laws encouraging small business and the middle class are justifiable functions of government. Invariably, such good laws will more than offset lost tax revenues by expanding the tax base. Good tax law for small businesses is sound economic policy for our government.

I have worked with minority and other business start-ups most of my career. In my experience as a CPA, there are five things which put small business start-ups out of business. With these shoestring start-up operations, inadequate initial working capital is a given; I won't even list it as a problem.

The Problem	The Solution
1. Payroll taxes.	Reformed tax policy.
2. The cost of insurance.	Insurance industry reform.
3. Bad management due to a lack of experience.	Freedom of choice in education and cradle-to-grave education.

4. Unfair competition and predatory pricing by big business.	Jeffersonian economic intervention and strengthening the Sherman Anti-Trust Act.
5. Lawyers, litigation, and other "red tape."	Tort reform and Jeffersonian interventions.

On this list, we have discussed all of these except insurance and insurance companies. The more I know about insurance the less I like it. But, I have to confess, I have not studied the insurance industry enough to intelligently propose reforms.

However, economic problems and solutions can be understood when you look at them in simple terms like the above table. Economics is not all that complex a subject. Just think, do you want to live in an American economy dominated by big businesses, or do you want the economy in the hands of the middle class and middle-class owned small business? Before you answer, remember that 75 percent of American jobs are in small businesses!

The economic goal I find most important is insuring equal access to the economy for all Americans. This policy will make the goal of substantially eradicating racial tensions in America possible. Equal access to the economy is an American dream too long denied to black citizens. The irony of freedom denied to some is that this traditional plight of the black community is now the issue for all of us: none of us are free unless all of us are free.

All that we have talked about in economic and tax reform will make it easier for blacks and all Americans to move into the middle class and continue to improve their economic status. Certainly, it makes it easier for a black family to start a small business when they can buy at the same wholesale prices enjoyed by Wal-Mart. Knocking economic barriers down helps everybody, except the very rich. I will not lose any sleep over the rich man, and neither did Lazarus.

Education reforms and economic and tax reforms move us closer to the goal but not close enough. We should avoid making laws that will allow the federal government to intervene in peoples' lives, even when they mean well. The American government is at its most dangerous when it means to do good. Giving people money on which to live will never cure their poverty. Month to month, the money runs out. Such laws are simply welfare by whatever other name they are called. One popular code name for welfare is redistribution of wealth. But, government-transacted redistribution of wealth does not make more wealth, nor does it make anyone more wealthy. In fact, it makes more people poor and keeps poor people locked into poverty.

However, making laws that encourage good things is a legitimate function of government. Equal access to the economy is a good thing. Moving people out of poverty into the middle class is a good thing. These economic policies cannot be called welfare for the simple reason that they create more wealth for more people. I like policies which produce these results. There is nothing wrong with the redistribution of wealth if it is done properly. But, the only valid way to accomplish this goal is through the private-sector economy creating more wealth for more people.

There are at least three barriers to equal access to the economy: education and know-how; a lack of capital; and, a lack of opportunities. These are three barriers that need to be knocked down flat.

Education and Know-How

I have been involved in many attempts to organize minority start-ups, and I have seen many failures and many successes. There are no short answers to understanding the failures or to insure repeated successes. The success or failure of a small business is a study unto itself. A well-done study of the successes or failures of minority-owned small businesses would likely earn me a Ph.D.

Two things have always struck me as important about small business start-ups. First, the personality type we call the entrepreneur is colorblind. When you read the literature about entrepreneurship and the personal characteristics of the entrepreneur, the personality traits will jump out at you. And, they are not all positive personality traits either.

These entrepreneur people tend to be smart, impatient, and a little arrogant at times. When things move too slowly, they get agitated. The entrepreneur does not like sideline quarterbacks telling him how to run his business. Further, the entrepreneur can be very hard to get along with; many start their own businesses because they keep getting fired. Bankers, lawyers, and accountants are quickly cast as sideline quarterbacks and, in general, agitate the entrepreneur. With personality traits like these, it is a wonder that entrepreneurs stay in business. Most don't; the failure rate for business start-ups is over 85 percent. With good law removing economic barriers, we can lower that rate some.

The second thing that I find compelling about small business start-ups is that a team of dedicated and experienced business professionals (sideline quarterbacks) assisting the entrepreneur improve the odds of success measurably. However, the failure rate for business start-ups will always be high.

Good Tax Laws Encouraging Capital Formation

Tax laws to encourage private capital formation specifically targeted at minority-owned and operated small businesses will be very helpful. I envision a special nongovernment-financed, minority small business start-up program written into law. A tax and capital formation program loaded with goodies, such as refundable tax credits on invested capital; an ordinary income deduction for any capital lost in minority start-up ventures *at twice the original investment;* and, unrestricted pass-through of initial losses to investors and the ability to direct those initial losses to investors by contractual agreement without regard to stock ownership or the ratios of invested capital.[2]

Such a program should have one critical restriction. A team of five dedicated and experienced business professionals must agree to assist the venture for a five-year minimum as the acting board of directors. The team must have a CPA, a lawyer, a banker, and two other successful business people, unrelated by blood or marriage to the entrepreneur. This team is paid for by the start-up business at their standard billing rates. Team members may also be investors, such as bankers, watchdogging their own investment. The purpose of this team is to educate and train the minority entrepreneur.

This team should see that at least the five following items are being professionally managed: (1) financial statements are produced each month including income statement, balance sheet, general ledger, necessary journals, payroll records, and bank reconciliations; (2) operating and production budgets and variance reports are developed each month; (3) continuous cash flow and credit needs projections are maintained, reviewed, and understood by the entrepreneur; (4) verify that all trust fund taxes and payroll taxes are properly accounted for and remitted; and, (5) develop and periodically review marketing plans.

This acting board of directors or management team is in effect providing necessary services to improve the probability of success for the start-up business and to also provide on-the-job training, or OJT, as some of my clients call it. This type of arrangement may chaff the typical entrepreneur given their volatile personality types, but sacrifices are necessary when anyone does business with other people's money. Invested capital is by definition just that, other people's money. Of course, if the minority entrepreneur does not like the arrangement, he or she can turn down the tax credits, financing, and double deductions on business losses.

Furthermore, entrepreneurial education does not stop there. Refundable tax credits should be allowed for all job training and professional, technical, or business education. I believe education is an important key to success. It is true that capitalism without the capital is just an–ism; however, it is also true that capital without know-how is a disaster!

Create Opportunities

Opportunities are important. In this day of American "restructuring" where the new big business Barons are "downsizing" and "creating market share," there are fewer opportunities for everyone.

You need a modern dictionary of business terms just to read that last sentence. *Restructuring* really means the economy is in chaos and can be translated as "business is bad and we don't know what else to do." It can also mean, "we're shutting factories and abandoning traditional markets." *Downsizing* means you or someone you know lost their job. And, *creating market share* means some big business is putting many small businesses permanently out of business with a pattern of predatory pricing. The goal is to eliminate competitors.

We also need more business opportunities. Because of the resurfacing of Robber Baron business tactics in our modern economy, there are too few business opportunities available. We need to create more. Disfranchising the Robber Barons by economic legislation will create a wealth of new opportunities.

We also need to downsize governments, make them more efficient, and reduce their cancerous demands for ever high rates of tax. It is the only way to kick government out of our economic lives. With planning, downsizing governments can create business opportunities.

I will only brush the surface of possibilities in privatization of government services. A concerted effort to privatize government will find many opportunities at all levels of local, state, and federal governments. We need such an effort to privatize government for two important reasons: to make government less expensive and to preserve maximum freedom for our people. Bigger government equals less freedom. Smaller government equals more freedom.

I believe that decentralized, free-market capitalism and private industry can do almost anything better than government bureaucrats. For example, garbage pick-up, police, fire, and paramedical services, tax collections, and administration all belong in private industry. Governments should grant the franchise rights to one or more qualified businesses. The franchisees must have a management team and meet certain standards such as the ones I've outlined earlier.

In times past, all these services were in the hands of small businesses. I admit, small business police franchisees would require special training and oversight and would never replace the much smaller public police forces charged to work with the private, franchised police in matters of training, investigations, and quality reviews. But, we still have at least one city with privately owned and operated police franchises.

Likewise, we need to downsize certain state government services. Education is at the top of my list as you already know. But, we also need to privatize prisons, hospitals, tax collections, tax audits, and a variety of other state services.

Prisons would be the most difficult service to privatize, yet there are a number of private prisons in America doing very well.

The inmate population has a better, more human environment; the state saves money; and the investors make a profit. The state department of prisons would be reduced to an oversight role charged with quality review and training.

There are so many opportunities to privatize the federal government that it is almost easier to list some of the services that should not be privatized: the military, the FBI, the Department of State, and the intelligence and national security agencies. But, even these listed services should downsize and privatize many of their functions.

A few operations of government that can be privatized are the IRS, the statistical and data gathering services of the Department of Education and the other cabinet-level departments, the Post Office, and much of the legal work of the various departments including the Department of Justice.

The Post Office will whine and tell you that their monopoly is necessary to deliver thirty-two cent mail to remote and rural areas. But, I will tell you that if the federal government sold nonexclusive franchise rights to carry all types of mail, with the stipulation that first-class letters have a uniform nationwide price, there would be no shortage of private businesses in the bidding. The obvious bidders are UPS, Federal Express, Airborne, Western Union, and a few others you may not expect. Privatizing the postal service is an excellent idea long overdue.

Privatizing the IRS would be a little more complex, but it is also a good idea. Examinations of all income, excises, and other tax returns should be done on a contract basis. We have six national CPA firms who could divvy up most of the workload. Even local CPA firms should be able to bid on tax examination work. The IRS role should be limited to auditing the auditors and processing tax returns. Even the quality review of the tax working papers could be done as a part of the peer review process, where one CPA firm audits another's work product. I can think of a number of private companies ready to jump on a contract as collectors of delinquent and overdue taxes.

Privatization is necessary and so is a systematic build-down of social programs in order to allow for lower taxes. Lower taxes are important. The lower our taxes, the more free the economy and our citizens. Many liberals would sharply disagree with me on this point. The liberal will tell you that our taxes are low compared to Europe. That's true. All of Western Europe is higher than U.S. taxation. Some European countries have tax burdens more than double our already heavy burden.

But, Europeans do not have the American traditions of freedom and Andy Jackson vintage self-reliance. To be coddled by their governments may make Europeans comfortable, but it chafes Americans. The European tradition of citizen reliance upon their governments has changed their society. Evangelical Christianity is dying in Europe due to the secularization of their society. America is also becoming more secular for the same reasons: citizen over-reliance upon a secular government. Extensive social programs undermines evangelical Christianity.

Also, this level of taxation has changed the European economy making them progressively less competitive. The cost of labor in Europe is much higher than in America due to taxes. European industries cannot compete on an equal footing with American industries for much longer. The gap in quality between American and European products is closing fast. For example, who is going to buy a Mercedes when you can buy a Ford Lincoln that is just as well engineered at half the cost. Europe is already relying on protectionist trade measures to block Japanese entry into their markets. In the future, Europe will rely on restraints in freedom of trade to protect them from the American and Asian economic juggernauts.

The American economy has more in common with Asia's economy than with Europe's. The Asian economy is taxed much less than the American economy, on average 10 to 15 percentage points less. Even Japan's economy, which is taxed at approximately the same as the American rate, avoids punitive tax policy. Instead of punitive tax policy to inhibit economic activity, Japan's policy encourages economic activity. For example, Japanese tax policy encourages business meals and entertainment. I admit, federal policy to discourage the use of restaurants irritates me. I see no possible economic logic to support this policy. Such a policy is merely political fodder to feed the election cycle.

America's economic future has three steps in the foreseeable future. First, rebuild American small business and plug small business into international markets. Second, use NAFTLA to create a zone of economic prosperity and political stability covering all of North America. Then, NAFTLA will be extended to the entire Western Hemisphere bringing with it the typical benefits of free trade and equal access to the economy. An increase in economic freedom is always accompanied by an increase in national wealth.

Lastly, these NAFTLA-created zones of economic prosperity and political stability then will be extended very slowly, one nation at a time into the Asian rim countries. Japan will come into a NAFTLA-style arrangement late, if at all. However, the non-Japanese Asian economy is much richer than any one nation, even Japan.

By exporting the American political doctrines of equal access to the economy and freedom in international trade, an expanding American economic power could pave a road to a richer, more stable world. The keys to this success are a low tax economy, a large and expanding middle class, and a significantly downsized government. A simple political agenda. This is a political agenda the Church can endorse.

This is also the direction America's freedoms should take, in my opinion. But, I am only one voice in the great debate that defines America. The Church, of which I am a part, has a much larger voice to be heard, a voice that must be free to express our views. If the political voice of the Church is repressed, by unconstitutional laws or by our own lack of patriotism, America will suffer. We will have failed our nation and the call of God on our Church.

Endnotes

1. Larry Burkett and Harry E. Figgie, Jr., both of whom I have previously mentioned, have written extensively about this possibility.

2. We double tax dividends, so a double tax deduction for capital losses of minority ventures is not more illogical than a double tax. Besides, whoever said tax law was logical! Surely not me.

CHAPTER TWELVE

A Reformed Church

There is no question that we need political and economic reforms in America. There is one other reform that we dare not overlook; we need reform in the American Church. Perhaps a better term than *reform* is *revival*. By whatever name, however, America needs more from her Church than she has yet to receive.

To my mind, there is little question that the Church is, and has been, a major contributing factor in every social problem facing our nation today. Not a cure, mind you, but a cause of trouble. Often we have been guilty of the sins of omission: apathy and negligence. These sins show Americans that the Church is without any semblance of Christ-like concern for others. At times, we have actually been guilty of active sins such as racism and materialism. By these sins we deny Christ, who knows no black or white, rich or poor, slave or free. It is time for the American Church to break through the evil that has so easily ensnared us and to reach out for all the good God intends for us (Heb. 12:1).

We can never know the extent of the evil that we ourselves have visited upon our nation: could the Church have cured the evil of pre-Civil War slavery without bloodshed? Could we have healed the nation without civil war? Could we have fed the poor in their times of need such as the Great Depression? Could we have worked for greater freedom in the struggle for civil rights? I believe we could have. If we had, America would now truly be a nation under God instead of a nation struggling to be a secular society, free of all forms of godliness. Yet, even now, we are still a nation committed to freedom and that hope which freedom brings. I believe in that hope, and, because of that hope, I believe America will overcome the evil we have visited upon her. And, I believe the Church will be critically important in this time of healing in America.

The Church, in its present condition, will lead us nowhere. We need much more than mere political and social changes in America. We need the leadership of a reformed Church. In effect, we need a revival.

Ironically, the way to spark a revival is also the beginning of healing for the land: "If my people, who are called by my name, will humble themselves and pray, I, the Lord, will heal their land" (2 Chron. 7:14). The only tool provided in Scripture to heal a nation is the Church, i.e., the "people who are called by my name." Due to our arrogance, through which the Church has visited much evil upon America, the healing God has for America has been unavailable. As with his tools of healing, God will only work with the humble who seek His will.

Nations, like men, can become arrogant. In America we have the twin problems of arrogance as a nation and as the Church. But, even in our arrogance, God loves us. Humility is required before we can recognize and admit to our own sins. God will only lead the humble who are willing to submit to His will. God will make opportunities for the proud and arrogant to find humility. God's love is awesome.

Revival cannot come if we are mired in sins. Some of our sins are generations old and yet to be confessed before the Lord. Without repentance and confession we cannot deal with our sins. Confession is easy. If we confess, God will forgive us. Our salvation is assured. However, it takes more than confession to deal with sin in our life; it takes repentance.

Billy Graham says that repentance is the turning away from sin and setting a new and godly course. Only a godly sorrow, caused by a painful awareness of our sins, will lead us to repentance (2 Cor. 7:9–10). Repentance is not complete until we can bring forth fruits worthy of our repentance, fruits that will show the world of our new course. Sweet fruits indeed!

Without repentance, Christians cannot rediscover their ethical foundation in the person of Jesus Christ. Revival depends upon this rediscovery. As Christ reminds us, ethics is simply acting out the teachings of Jesus: "If ye love me, keep my commandments" (John 14:15).

No revival anywhere, at anytime, has happened without God's people being on their knees in seasons of prayer. Humility will drive you to your knees. So will repentance. So will pain. In times of prayer, we heal our own soul, and we become stronger in faith. We can also heal our churches, making them stronger in the Lord. If enough of us pray, we can heal the whole Church. And, when the Church begins to heal, revival happens.

On our knees in prayer we are powerful because we effectively deal with those sins which hinder our faith. That is why the greatest battles between good and evil are fought on our knees in prayer. Prayer is merely removing self-imposed barriers between us and God. Standing before God brings healing to us and to all around us. It makes our faith strong. Only by humbly standing before the Creator in repentance can any of us be remade righteous: "Confess your faults one to another, and pray one for another, that ye may be healed. The effectual fervent prayer of a righteous man availeth much" (James 5:16).

When we truly stand before God in prayer, all we will want is what God wants for us. There is no room for selfishness. Certainly no room for prayers that are a mere laundry list of "I wants." When we stand before God, there is only room for God. Everything but God is pushed out of our lives, and only God remains. In this way, prayer cleanses the soul. Such prayer can be painful and scary as we let go of everything and face God alone. However, it is the only way we can ever know God. To know God is to want everything He wants for you.

When we truly want what God wants, we can ask for anything, and we will receive it (Matt. 21:22; Phil. 4:6). If the Church agrees together, in prayer, there is no limit to what we can accomplish (see Matt. 18:19–20 and John 14:13–14). We can surely save America. In Christ, the American Church can save the world.

Revival only comes when God's spirit is allowed to fill the hearts of His people. The only containers in all of creation able to be filled with such an outpouring are the hearts of Christians, open and ready to receive the Lord. Revival always begins with a season of prayer, is followed by an outpouring of the Holy Spirit, and always ends with a nation being blessed (see Acts 1:14; 2:1– 4, 37–47). America needs an outpouring of the Holy Spirit.

God is not a miser to be convinced or begged into an outpouring of His Holy Spirit. God is, and always has been, ready to pour out a blessing on His Church the likes of which we cannot contain. Therein lies the obstacle that prevents revival: our container (our hearts) is far too small. The limiting factor to revival is not God, it is us (Luke 11:13). We need to make our hearts bigger through love and generosity. God has asked us to do precisely that—make our hearts grow bigger by practicing His agape love.

I believe we are already entering a season of revival in America. Some call it a spirit of renewal in the Church, others an outpouring of God's spirit on America. I call it the old-old story, as old as time. In Scripture, and all throughout history, when people returned to God in repentance and faith, renewal came. God's spirit begins to work when hearts are ready to receive the gift of the Spirit of God. Revival breaks out when people turn to God.

God never abandons His people. People abandon God. By simply returning to God we can gain access to the power that created the universe. What we forfeit by our disobedience is beyond comprehension. Revival is simply removing self-imposed roadblocks so we can gain access to God.

Revival is always accomplished with a sense of joy, a heart of forgiveness, love overflowing, and a spirit of giving. There is always an overwhelming desire to bring God's healing to the land. God's harsh judgment often precedes revival as God helps us understand our need for humility. Revival is a time for God to heal nations. The humility of the Church is a small price to pay for healing a nation.

I see evidence that revival is beginning. Living Waters Church, a tiny congregation in rural Alabama, is leading its own quiet revival by their dedication to a single ministry of healing called the Canaan Land Girls Home. Pray for Peace Ministries has extraordinary welfare ministries that benefits two great nations, America and Russia. Christ the King Church is a modest size local congregation that feeds and clothes the poor, provides homes for the homeless, and healing for the sick. They even have a church-sponsored reform school for adolescents with behavior problems. These humble ministries are laying the groundwork for, and defining the nature of, the next great American revival.

These ministries all have several things in common. One is that they do not see themselves as extraordinary. In fact, they think they're normal. It is my prayer that one day this level of Christian achievement in the Church will be seen as normal. These people have captured the heart and soul of Christianity. They are indeed the Church. Another thing they share is an ethical commitment as Christians that breaks the yokes of slavery and brings hope to the hopeless. Above all else, they share the kind of Christian love that is unmistakable, unmatchable, and clearly from God. This agape love drives them to godly actions. I stand in awe of them.

In their own quiet way, these heroes of the faith, and many others like them, are changing forever the nature of the American Church. Praise God! We need to bring this kind of revival home.

God has brought us to the point of revival. God's ever gentle judgment upon the Church has made us humble. We need humility before God can exalt us (1 Pet. 5:6). Gently, God has shown us the godless condition of our nation and the consequences of godlessness. Daily we are made aware that society does not want, nor feel they need, our help in healing the land. Our godly agenda is seen as conservative, part of the problem, and not a pathway to social solutions.

In this condemnation, our nation is telling us that we must share the blame for society's tragic condition. We have every reason in the world to be humbled by this condemnation and no reason whatsoever for arrogance. Our Constitution, our Lord, and the Scriptures all tell us that the Church is responsible for the moral welfare of our nation. Look at what we have done with this holy responsibility and know beyond any doubt that we have reason to be humble. To put it most simply, we, the Church, have failed.

The only hope we have to save America is for a new outpouring of God's spirit. There is a new spirit sweeping the Church in our land. The Holy Spirit is calling us to a renewal and a return to the basics of our faith: love, hope, and freedom. In this, the truth shall surely set us free. It is the only way we will ever be free.

A compelling result of revival is the salvation of souls. The first revival in Scripture won three thousand souls in one day (Acts 2:47)! We need revival to get on with the business of saving souls.

One of the benefits of the first revival, recorded in Acts, was that the Christians brought together their material resources for the purpose of ministering to the needy. The ministry of giving to people's material needs is always a direct result of revival. Revival causes people to be generous and to act in accordance with the Word of God. God's Word is clear: we must be a generous people.

America needs a true revival because millions of people live in desperate poverty, and government-sponsored solutions have failed miserably. We are called by God to break every yoke of slavery. Poverty is one yoke that we must actively work to break if we are to survive as a free nation. America must have welfare reform that will lift people out of slavery. That reform can only come from the Church.

Our current government-sponsored welfare system perpetrates a cycle of poverty that is almost unbreakable. The Church cannot stand by while our own government, well intended or otherwise, forces people into this new slavery called welfare. Slavery, by whatever name, is evil. Slavery cannot be indefinitely maintained; it will eventually explode into hatred, anger, and violence. This explosion has already begun.

It is unthinkable for the Church to allow a modern slavery to trap generation after generation of mostly black citizens in poverty. America tried slavery once and paid for the error in blood. America, as a nation, almost died in civil war caused by the sin of slavery. Slavery will always erupt into violence. This time, if this new form of slavery is allowed to persist, America will not survive.

In a time of revival we can see old problems with a new and godly vision. America has serious problems that threaten our very existence as a nation. These problems can overwhelm those who have too little faith. I believe in America: not only will we survive, I believe we will prosper. Our problems are real and deadly serious. They have already erupted into violence and will likely do so again. This is not a situation conducive to optimism, yet, I remain confident that America will not fail.

Bill Moyer, a well-known newscaster, reported recently that our nation's leaders, Republicans and Democrats alike, have little hope for our future as a nation. The economic and social problems we face have spooked our political leaders. They can only see the death of the American dream. Likewise, many Christian and secular books about our future also focus on "doom and gloom." I disagree.

America, all through her short history, is a nation committed to a steady upward march to ever greater levels of freedom. We have a culture of freedom that will not be sacrificed in times of trouble. A nation committed to freedom is close to the heart of God.

For freedom's sake, God truly loves America, and whom God loves, He will correct (Heb. 12:6). God's correction is a humbling experience for a nation, just as it is for a man. God's correction, even though it may be harsh, is good, if America learns to humble herself. Humility may lead a nation to prayer and repentance. Only revival can save America. I believe God is engineering revival at this very moment. I believe America will be saved.

Revival will make the Church keenly interested in all that affects our nation. Economics and politics will be no exception. Revival will compel many Christians into political action. As I have predicted already in this book, I believe the most significant reform coming out of revival will be true welfare reform.

Privatizing the welfare system may be the only hope we have to break the yoke of slavery called poverty. Our current welfare system traps people in a multigenerational cycle of poverty. This demonic cycle is a yoke of slavery that robs millions of people of any hope. It is a yoke the Church should help break.

A private sector-sponsored welfare system, in which the church will be a significant participant, will have incredible advantages over the current bureaucratic nightmare in place. The cost of savings alone would be huge.

Funding a nationwide welfare ministry can be easily accomplished with John Kennedy-type tax reform. Dollar for dollar refundable tax credits, for up to 10 percent of taxable income, can be used to encourage charitable contributions to the private sector.

In addition, a private sector welfare system would be more productive in permanently lifting people out of poverty. Aid from your neighbors, who are interested in helping you, is a positive relationship for everyone. Aid from the government becomes an entitlement, a right. Entitlements destroy self-motivation. Therein lies the roots of poverty and apathy that is destroying people. Only private control of the welfare system can break this entitlement attitude.

There is one remarkable, unspoken factor that convinces me that privatization of the welfare system would be successful: the generous nature of the American people. Americans will not allow children to suffer once they are made aware of the needs, if they understand it is their personal responsibility. Generous money will flow to the real welfare needs. A little bit of a tax-motivated kicker will speed this generosity along.

American Christians have always had some sense of ethics concerning politics. For example, it is presumed that, as a minimum, Christians should vote. Unfortunately, our ethics have been limited.

Political actions that grow out of a spirit of revival must be based upon our long forgotten ethical standards for the Church: hope for the hopeless and breaking every yoke of slavery. Rediscovering our ethical foundations will be difficult. We must return to the root of our ethical foundation, Jesus. Jesus Christ must be the director and motivator of any concerted movement of the Church, especially a political movement. A Christian movement built upon such a foundation will not fail.

We need Christian leaders to show us the way; however, we do not need new personality cults. Personality cults and single issue politics are not appropriate for the Church. Good politics is having a well-defined, broad political agenda consistently presented over time. Our focusing on single issues has undermined the Church's impact in the political process and crippled our moral leadership in society. It hasn't helped restore our ethics either.

The Church's political movements can no longer be confined to mere labels, such as the liberal black churches or the so-called

Christian Right. We need to politically embrace all Christians fundamentally committed to the ministries of hope and freedom. Evangelical conservatives, liberal blacks, and other diverse labels become less important than the agenda of hope for the hopeless and the eradication of all forms of slavery in our land.

God called the Church to be both salt and light. Our society is in decay; our salt is the preservative to stop this decay. We live in a society made dark by violence, immorality, ignorance, poverty, and so many other sins. Light drives out darkness. God has called us to be both salt and light for America. We can do no less and still honor God.

Jesus tried to explain all of this to us. Announced at the beginning of His earthly ministry, Jesus stood in the synagogue and quoted Isaiah's prophecy:

> The Spirit of the Lord is upon Me,
> Because He anointed Me to preach the gospel to the poor.
> He has sent Me to proclaim release to the captives,
> And recovery of sight to the blind,
> To set free those who are downtrodden,
> to proclaim the favorable year of the Lord. (Luke 4:18–19)

Jesus came to make us free. There is no ministry more necessary or more noble for the American Church than this ministry given to us by Christ Himself.

Freedom! Freedom! Freedom! In God's name, I love that word *freedom.*

A Summary of Important Legal Cases with Implications for the Church

The *Bob Jones University v. U.S.* Case

The Supreme Court conceded that Mr. Jones had a sincerely held conviction of religious faith protected by the First Amendment. But Bob Jones' sincerely held conviction of his faith could not be protected when the organization is in receipt of a federal financial subsidy[1] and the conviction of faith is contrary to clearly stated public policy. Clearly stated public policy is, according to the Supreme Court, more important than the First Amendment.

The Bob Jones case created important new constitutional law. The concept that a church or other religious organization must conform to standards of "clearly stated public policy" is important new law created by the Bob Jones case. From the point of view of the IRS and the United States Justice Department, Bob Jones was an ideal case.

The facts in the Bob Jones case are simple. Bob Jones University, a tax exempt 501(c)(3) organization, has rules for student conduct. One of these rules was a clear statement that the university believed the Bible taught against interracial dating and marriage. Interracial dating and marriage was therefore forbidden. Never once was this rule enforced by Bob Jones University; apparently the rule was never violated by the students. It was stipulated (agreed to by all parties concerned) that Bob Jones and Bob Jones University had a "sincerely held conviction of faith protected by the First Amendment." There is no question that Bob Jones was an effort on the part of the IRS and the United States Justice Department to create important new police powers to be used against First Amendment-protected organizations such as churches.

It's not easy to make new law

The Supreme Court resists making new law. The popular press has many people believing that the Justices on the Supreme Court actively look for opportunities to change the Constitution, create new legal theories, and blaze new legal trails. This popular perception is wrong. Contrary to creating new law, the Justices on the Supreme Court strongly prefer to rely on prior cases and legal precedents. This reliance on prior legal precedent causes the Supreme Court to be far more conservative in nature than the individual Justices that sit on the Court.[2] Any attempt to making new constitutional law is difficult.

The Perfect Case

Before the IRS could hope to win, they needed the perfect case. Bob Jones was a perfect case to overturn two hundred years of law. To some degree, Dr. Bob Jones and Bob Jones University suffered from being in the wrong time in history with the wrong facts.

What defeated Bob Jones was a charge of "Racial Discrimination." When the courts finished with the case it was expanded to include "other public policy violations." Our society has evolved from a past of slavery and is hopefully going to a future where all people are truly free. We are not there yet; we are somewhere in the middle where racial discrimination is a fact. Merely making the charge of racial discrimination against anybody creates an atmosphere of intense shame and suspicion. More than that, the mere charge of racial discrimination creates a presumption of guilt against the accused.[3] The presumption of guilt against Bob Jones was overwhelming; Bob Jones was defeated long before his case came to stand before the Supreme Court.

Dr. Bob Jones is a brilliant, well-educated man of God. In any discussion of discrimination, the first thing to jump into the mind of Dr. Bob Jones would likely be "no Greek or Jew, no slave or free."[4] His religious education and training would have made it impossible for Dr. Bob Jones to intentionally discriminate against anyone on the basis of race.[5] Not a single student at Bob Jones University believed he or she was the target of racial discrimination. The students with whom Bob Jones worked never accused him of anything so heinous as racial discrimination. Black students of Bob Jones University, in court room testimonies and statements to the press, were unanimous in their praise of Dr. Bob Jones and Bob Jones University. Even the NAACP filed a brief with the Supreme Court opposing the IRS's position in the Bob Jones case!

I personally believe Dr. Bob Jones made a serious political and theological error in proposing rules against interracial dating and marriage. I also believe that Bob Jones never intended to unfairly discriminate against anyone. The idea of unfair discrimination based upon race is totally alien to sound Christian theology and the Word of God.

These facts are interesting:

Dr. Jones was supported by his students, both black and white.

Dr. Jones' superior religious education and training would have made intentional acts of discrimination unlikely.

Dr. Jones received widespread support in both the Christian and civil rights communities.

Such facts point to the mind and heart of Dr. Bob Jones and the administrators of Bob Jones University. However interesting these facts may be, they do not change the central truth in the Bob Jones case. The truth is that Bob Jones University had rules that were based upon race. By definition, such rules inherently discriminate. Our society finds such rules, based upon race, to be offensive.

Our political and judicial leaders intend to eradicate anything hinting of discrimination. In their zeal to do good, many Christian and other good institutions have been and will be hurt. When the Constitution's meaning is changed, the damage may not be fully realized for generations.

The Hidden Agenda

It takes a highly inflammatory issue, such as racial discrimination, to make the Supreme Court change the meaning of the

Constitution of the United States. Ironically, the real issue in Bob Jones was not about racial discrimination or even the heart and intentions of Dr. Bob Jones. The real issue was how to give the federal government additional power to work around the First Amendment to the Constitution of the United States so the IRS could "police" heretofore protected churches and religious organizations. The conclusions of the Supreme Court in Bob Jones gave the federal government new police powers to regulate churches and religious organizations. More "police powers," by default, means less freedom. Stipulated convictions of faith, protected by this precious Bill of Rights notwithstanding, the First Amendment was dealt a serious blow.

The Supreme Court held that religious organizations must provide a "public benefit" and conform to current standards of "public policy." This is a "compelling interest" which overrides any burden that denial of tax benefits may have on the "free exercise of religion."[6] Racial discrimination was the flash point in having the First Amendment's protections radically reinterpreted.

Few Americans disagree with this result when the issue at conflict with the First Amendment is racial discrimination. However, the idea that the church must now, by law, maintain new standards in support of "clearly stated public policy" will hang like the proverbial "mill stone" around our necks.

Most well-educated and well-trained Christians today agree that eradication of racial discrimination is a godly goal; consistent with the Word of God and the will of God. Unfortunately, the implications of Bob Jones go far beyond racial discrimination.

The Supreme Court Made a Mistake

There are three serious logical flaws in the Court's reasoning in this line of trend-setting case.

1. The new legal standards to which the Church must support:

"Clearly stated public policy,"

"Common community Standards,"

"Provide for a public benefit,"

in effect, require all religious organizations to conform to standards other than the Word of God. This new standard may be called "political correctness in religion."

2. Unlike God, who is unchanging, these new legal standards are fickle. They change over time. In fact, they change radically and quickly.

3. These new legal standards grant the federal government vast new police powers. Apparently the police agency selected to exercise this enormous new constitutional power is the IRS. Giving the IRS more power makes me nervous. I believe the IRS has too much power already. They scare me.

I mark the 1983 Bob Jones case as the day the First Amendment died. The 1962 case of *Engel v. Vitale,* mortally wounded the First Amendment. The final death knell was the Bob Jones case.

The *Engel v. Vitale* Case

The *Engel v. Vitale* case turned the entire meaning of the First Amendment upside down. Prior to this 1962 case, the Establishment clause was clearly meant to restrict the federal government in any attempt to "establish a national denomination."

The First Amendment: To protect the people

The First Amendment, like all of the first Ten Amendments to the Constitution contained in the Bill of Rights were assumed to be a restriction on Congress and the government, not restriction on the people. However, after 1962, the *Engel v. Vitale* case reinterpreted the Establishment clause of the First Amendment to be a restriction on the "religious activities" of the people.

The First Amendment: A weapon against the people

The phrase "separation between Church and State"[7] was never intended by our founding Fathers to have the meaning given it by the *Engel v. Vitale* case. It is tragic that the people's Bill of Rights has been twisted to the point where it is now being used by our government against the people. *Engel v. Vitale* and subsequent cases along the same line of reasoning so weakened the First Amendment that a case like Bob Jones became inevitable.

Immediately on the heels of Bob Jones we had another blow to the First Amendment.[8] Shortly after the Bob Jones case became the "Law of the Land," I made several dozen speeches in churches and to other groups. In these speeches I stated that when the First Amendment's religious protections clauses died, the free speech provision of the First Amendment would not be far behind. Unfortunately, I may have been more prophetic than I knew.

Community Standards Always Change

The most important reality of the Bob Jones doctrine is that all tax-exempt religious organizations must conform to acceptable community standards in their conduct. Community standards change continually. Changes in acceptable community standards are not always good. Many recent changes in community standards violate our Christian beliefs.

Community standards seem to deteriorate daily. To study how community standards change, I am going to take a closer look at homosexual rights. I choose homosexual rights merely because they are today's hot issue.[9] In many other ways, not related to homosexuality, community standards are also eroding. When community standards begin to decline, the slip can turn into an avalanche!

Community standards affect all Americans. It affects our nation's morality. It influences our work ethic and how loyal we are to our employers, how diligent we work at our jobs, etc. Community standards govern attitudes of how we manage debt and spend our money. Community standards even impact how we use our courts. America has been called the most litigious society in the history of man. This degrading trend in community standards will have an undeniable impact on every aspect of American life.

The *Love* Case

The state of Massachusetts in September of 1993 took a major step in an effort to redefine what is morally acceptable in our society. The case involved a homosexual couple, prominent surgeons Dr. Susan Love and her lesbian lover of more than ten years, Dr. Helen Cooksey, whom allowed to adopt a five-year-old girl. Before September of 1993, such an adoption by a lesbian was unthinkable for obvious reasons. Because of the actions of the state of Massachusetts, a crack in the dam of acceptable community conscience has appeared and will grow to a flood over time.

Definitions of right and wrong in the "common community conscience" change as our society's morality changes with the times.

The 1993 Massachusetts Supreme Court case demonstrates that government is active in defining what is in the public interest. By doing so, government participates in redefining what is acceptable in the "common community conscience."

Our government is active in efforts to make equal rights for homosexuals normal and acceptable. The federal issues of homosexuals in the military and the Massachusetts adoption case redefining lesbian lovers as acceptable parents are merely the tip of a huge body of prohomosexual initiatives in our nation.

Equal rights for homosexuals is not currently acceptable in the "common community conscience." However, homosexual conduct may become accepted behavior due to the pressure government and prohomosexual special interest groups are applying to the courts, media, legislatures, and a variety of other means. Dr. Susan Love and her lesbian lover, Dr. Helen Cooksey, had the perfect case with which to make new prohomosexual rights law. Doctors Love and Cooksey set out a prohomosexual agenda with the intent of creating new law supporting their position. The five-year-old girl in the Love adoption case was the child of Dr. Cooksey via artificial insemination. Doctors Love and Cooksey raised this child from birth.

The court created new law based upon these two facts: the desires and rights of a natural birth mother and the five-year-long parental relationship between the child and Dr. Love. The desires and rights of the natural birth mother have powerful legal standing. Likewise, legal relationships are established by long-term parenting of a child—relationships in which any court is loathed to interfere. Existing powerful legal relationships are used to create new prohomosexual rights. By one more step, this case has changed our community standards.

Community Standards Affect All Americans

Uninformed people may believe, given these unique facts, that the court acted properly for the welfare of the child. The welfare of the child was not the legal issue in the Love case. The legal act of adoption will not give this child any new legal rights not already being provided by both Love and Cooksey. Both are physicians; either of the doctors is economically capable of providing all of the child's material and financial needs. In the court documents, both Love and Cooksey went to great lengths to demonstrate that they provided an emotionally supportive environment to a child they loved. The mere action of adoption does not give this child anything not already in place or available via other legal means, such as educational trust, support agreements, etc.

The purpose of the Love case was not to protect the child's welfare but was clearly an act by militant homosexuals to push the legal limits of homosexual rights. The facts in the case were perfect to accomplish their goal—and they won!

This case is important to Christians because it forever changes the definition of acceptable community standards. Our organizations are legally bound to these standards. Now, the federal government is limiting the church's input in the creation of these standards. Religious organizations are being shut out of the political process by the unconstitutional behavior of the IRS.

Endnotes

1. The theory of "tax expenditure analysis," as far as the Supreme Court is concerned, establishes that any church or other nonprofit organization is "subsidized" by the federal government.

2. An Associated Press (AP) wire report, dated Wednesday, 30 June 1993, carried the headline "High Court Term Showed a Lean to the Right."

3. The presumption of guilt in all charges of racial discrimination was made a part of our law by the IRS in Revenue Procedure 75-50. Concerning private community school, the IRS says, "The Service will consider these schools to be racially discriminatory." Guilty until proven innocent!

4. Galatians 3:28. For additional Scriptural guidance on discrimination, see the following:

Romans 10:12: "For there is no difference between the Jew and the Greek: for the same Lord over all is rich unto all that call upon him."

Colossians 3:11: "Where there is neither Greek nor Jew, circumcision nor uncircumcision, Barbarian, Scythian, bond nor free: but Christ is all, and in all."

5. Scriptural guidance dealing with discrimination.

Romans 2:11: "For there is no respect of persons with God."

Ephesians 6:9: "And, ye masters, do the same things unto them, forbearing threatening: knowing that your Master also is in heaven; neither is there respect of persons with him."

Colossians 3:25: "But he that doeth wrong shall receive for the wrong which he hath done: and there is no respect of persons."

James 2:1: "My brethren, have not the faith of our Lord Jesus Christ, the Lord of glory, with respect of persons."

James 2:9: "But if ye have respect to persons, ye commit sin, and are convinced of the law as transgressors."

6. *Bob Jones University v. US.* Applying this standard, the Supreme Court held that racially discriminatory educational institutions cannot be viewed as conferring a public benefit for purposes of the charitable deduction and that the government has a fundamental and compelling interest in eradicating racial discrimination in education which overrides the burden that denial of tax benefits may have on the free exercise of religion. See also *Jackson v. Statler Found, McGlotten v. Connally, Green v. Connally, Coit v. Green;* Rev Rul 71-447, 1971-2 CB 230; Rev Rul 75-231, 1975-1 CB 158; Rev Proc 75-50, 1975-2 CB 587.

7. The language, "separation between Church and State," appears nowhere in our Constitution or the Amendments thereto. The words were first used by Thomas Jefferson in a letter to the Baptists of New Hampshire to assure them that the Congregationalist Denomination nor any other denomination could ever be made national religious denominations. Jefferson said that Congress did not have that power because a "wall of separation exists between Church and State."

8. "First Amendment, RIP," Wednesday, 7 December 1983, headline in the *Washington Times.* This article was about the famous Nebraska "Ten" case. It began with an unforgettable first sentence, "Today, 10 Americans flee religious persecution—in America."

9. I do not want to minimize the sin of homosexual conduct. The Bible's teachings on the subject are clear: Romans 1:26 to Romans 1:32 present a biting indictment of the homosexual lifestyle. To me the most compelling verse is Romans 1:32, "Who knowing the judgment of God, that they which commit such things are worthy of death, not only do the same, but have pleasure in them that do them."

The IRS's View: Who Is an Independent Contractor and Who Is an Employee?

Recently I had an up-close and very personal look at raw IRS power. I was privileged to serve as an "expert" witness in an IRS tax case involving a logging contractor in Alabama who had been forced into bankruptcy, partly because of the IRS. An "expert" witness in a tax case is one who has an in-depth knowledge of the tax law and practice in a very narrow area. My narrow area of expertise is that I understand the specific issues involved in who is an independent contractor and who is an employee.

Thankfully, the man who was on trial was not my client. I do the best I can to keep my clients out of this kind of trouble. I was asked to serve as a witness by my dear friend and lawyer, Bruce Ely. Incidentally, I do not know of a better tax lawyer anywhere. When real tax money is on the table, I always work with Bruce.

The issue was employee versus self-employed status of loggers in the West Alabama region. The IRS sued the logging contractor for $161,000 of back payroll taxes. We won! My testimony was critical in turning a mere win into a full blown route of the IRS. We are now considering filing a claim with the court for reimbursement of our attorney and expert witness fees.

The IRS had no case whatsoever. Their case was trivial, entirely without merit. Long-standing custom in the logging industry, written contracts with workers, and pretrial testimony by 98 percent of the workers that they believed they were, and should be, treated as self-employed, were to no effect with the IRS. All of the facts and circumstances indicated that a logger is and should be treated as an independent contractor. The IRS knew all these facts before the trial even began, yet the IRS chose to proceed with this case.

The apparent reason the IRS litigated the case was to terrorize the West Alabama logging industry into compliance with the IRS's position. The real battle was one to inflict terror. The IRS won that battle! The IRS has succeeded in terrorizing many loggers in the West Alabama community into filing W-2 Forms. This man's legal and expert witness fees were in excess of forty-five thousand dollars. He's never made more than twenty thousand dollars a year in his life! Financially, he will never recover. In order to make a point, the IRS intentionally destroyed this man personally and professionally.

Given these facts, we can only conclude one thing: in this case, the IRS was not so much interested in obeying or applying the law, but in expanding their bureaucratic authority into the economic life of West Alabama. That frightens me! When law is used for any reason other than to see justice done, it is a frightening experience. If the IRS can't beat you at law, they will beat you with might and money. Either way, you get beat.

Oddly enough, at law and in court, our CPA firm has always won against the IRS. We have never had a loss to the IRS in court. But, I am very much afraid of the IRS. I do not want my clients to go to court with the IRS if court is avoidable.

The position of the IRS is that nearly everyone currently treated as an independent contractor, is really an employee and should get a W-2 Form, unless they work for many different employers and advertise their services to the general public or have statutory protection in the Internal Revenue Code. Before you decide to take on the IRS by adoption of a position contrary to the stated IRS position, count the costs. The cost of a fight with the IRS in court may be too expensive—even if you win.

If you use independent contractors in your business we need to take a fresh look at the ramifications of that decision. The IRS has announced a major crackdown on the issue of independent contractor versus employee status. There are many aspects of this crackdown. I will list a few:

1. The IRS will audit any individual who is issued Form 1099s by three or fewer employers.

2. The IRS will then audit the employers who issued the 1099s.

3. The IRS has publicly announced that it will use repeated IRS audits to convince people to treat their workers as employees. The IRS intends to frighten people and they say so publicly. The threat of an IRS audit can be very convincing.

4. This matter of who is an independent contractor and who is an employee has been given a high priority within the IRS. Money, manpower, and training have been poured into this issue by the IRS, at the urging of Congress and the General Accounting Office.

5. IRS agents have been given instructions to raise this issue on every audit, no matter what transactions triggered the audit.

My clients expect me to win against the IRS, not lose. Bruce Ely and I both believe that we will win and keep on winning most every legal battle over this issue of who is an independent contractor and who is an employee. But we also believe that we will lose the war. It boils down to this simple fact: if the IRS can't beat the employers of America using the law, they will beat them with might, money, and the terror of one IRS audit after another.

Either way, the citizen taxpayer will lose; as a CPA I cannot allow that to happen to my clients. We hope that each of our clients who use independent contractors will allow us to verify the legal protections available via the case law or the safe haven offered in section 530 of the Internal Revenue Code and assess the potential damage of continuing that position. Please call us for an appointment if you would like for us to review your situation.

A Letter to the Social Security Administration

Steve Richardson & Company
Certified Public Accountants, P. C.
Church Services Division

Steve Richardson, CPA	David R. Allison
President	Executive Director

September 23, 1993

Department of Health and Human Services
Social Security Administration
Southeastern Program Service Center
2001 Twelfth Avenue North
Birmingham, AL 35285

ATT: Carolyn Public Servant

RE: Taxpayer: Joe R. Taxpayer
     Identification Number: 123-45-6789 A

Dear Mrs. Servant:

Enclosed, for your convenience, is a copy of your letter dated September 22, 1993.

This customer is justifiably livid. This is the fourth time in four months that this client or his spouse has received mail from the

Social Security Administration suggesting error in the way he has reported wages to the Social Security Administration. In each case this client was assured that the misunderstanding had been corrected and all the problems had been resolved to the client's satisfaction only to receive another letter requesting data on exactly the same situation! This must stop!

This client cannot continue to pay me $100 an hour to fix an internal Social Security Administration problem; he can't afford to pay for your mistakes.

I have attached copies of prior correspondence and copies of internal Social Security Administration memos which "resolved" the problem in the past.

The problem is the way the IRS reports church wages to the Social Security Administration. The IRS counts W-2 wages as Social Security even when the wages are exempt from Social Security wages under Internal Revenue Code 3121(s) and must be counted as SE-Income on IRS Form 1040-SE. Then the IRS also reports SE-Income as Social Security earnings thereby double counting Social Security earnings. The problem is the lack of communications between the IRS and the Social Security Administration.

About two years ago the IRS fundamentally changed its procedures relative to the compensation practices of the Church. Ministers were no longer allowed to report earnings on Schedule C. Schedule C feeds data directly to Schedule SE and avoids this double counting which is the root of your Administration's internal trouble with Mr. Joe R. Taxpayer.

We have explained this carefully to the Social Security Administration on three prior occasions. We even have a memo in our files from the Social Security Administration verifying that we have corrected the problem. Why do I have the impression that we are dealing with a bureaucratic snarl where one person is unaware of the problem solving activities of another. This entire situation upsets me.

Please let me restate our case. This taxpayer earned $7,586 in Social Security earnings—not $13,097 as your records indicate.

Your records are wrong. We have shown Group 13 where and how this error was made by the IRS and the Social Security Administration. The error was not made by the taxpayer.

Attached please find a copy of the Taxpayer's W-2 Form from Cornerstone Baptist Church. This is the same W-2 that the Social Security Administration has looked at on three prior occasions. Please note that boxes 11, 12, 13, and 14 are all marked "EXEMPT." These boxes all relate to social security taxes or wages. The word *exempt* means do not factor this into your calculations.

	IRS & Social Security Administration's Calculations	True and correct Calculations
Tuscaloosa County Board of Education W-2 Form:	$2,467	$2,467
Cornerstone Baptist Church W-2 Form:	$6,000	$0
SE Taxable income from Cornerstone Baptist Church's W-2 Form:	$6,000	$6,000
SE Taxable income (loss) from Schedule C, lawn care business:	(457)	(457)
Statutory Discount on IRS Form Schedule SE:	(424)	(424)
Unexplained anomaly in Social Security Administration's calculations	(489)	N/A
Totals	$13,097	$7,586

Mrs. Servant, I am sure you understand why Mr. Taxpayer and I are upset about this. This is the fourth time we have had to deal with this. We cured the problem in 1991 and now must re-cure the problem in 1992. Is Mr. Taxpayer going to be forced to cure the problem again in 1993, 1994 and each year until his death. This is not Mr. Taxpayer's problem to cure.

The problem is a communications error between the Social Security Administration and the IRS. I am sure you have some means of correcting the communications breakdown. Please make every effort to do so.

Please do not hesitate to call me if I may be of assistance to you in this matter. I hold valid power of attorney, on file with the Social Security Administration; unless, of course, you've lost that too.

Sincerely,

Steve Richardson, CPA
For the Firm

cc   Joe R. Taxpayer
        123 Elm Street
        Heart of Dixie Alabama

The IRS's Double-Speak Letter

The Honorable Richard C. Shelby
Washington, D.C. 20515

Dear Mr. Shelby:

This is in further response to your communication dated January 31, 1984, on behalf of Mr. Steve Richardson, CPA, regarding his objections to the Internal Revenue Service's authority to determine the status of an ordaining church.

Mr. Richardson's objection is due to a request for information from the Service to a minister who is requesting exemption from self-employment tax under section 1402(e) of the Internal Revenue Code.

Under section 1402(e) of the Code an ordained, commissioned, or licensed minister is eligible for the exemption from self-employment tax if the minister is able to establish that the church which ordained, commissioned, or licensed him is described in sections 501(c)(3) and 170(b)(1)(A)(i) of the Code. We are enclosing copies of Revenue Rulings 76-415 and 80-59, for your examination. Neither revenue ruling requires the church to file for and be recognized as exempt from federal income tax for purposes of the section 1402(e) exemption.

Section 508(c)(1)(A) of the Code specifically excepts churches from the filing requirements that other organizations are subject to. Churches are treated as exempt from federal income tax even if they choose not to file an application for recognition of exemption from federal income tax. Accordingly, the Service does not establish the validity of a church. However, in order for an individual to be entitled to the benefits that flow from affiliation with an organization treated as exempt, such as exemption from self-employment tax, the individual must provide information to show that the church is described in sections 501(c)(3) and 170(b)(1)(A)(i).

We hope this helps you in providing information to your constituent.

Sincerely yours,

Ima IRS Bosslady
Chief, Exempt Organizations
Ruling Branch

Determining Church Status

Because the Internal Revenue Code fails to provide a verbatim definition of a church, the IRS developed a list of fourteen "criteria" which, at least in their estimation, characterize a church. These criteria have been used and recognized by the courts in a number of cases involving churches.[1]

1. Legal Existence: Your church must have a definite legal existence with the Articles of Incorporation. You have a Certificate of Incorporation provided by the Secretary of State. Please see additional comments under the section, "Legal Entity."

2. Officially Recognized Creed and Form of Worship: Your church should have an officially recognized creed (statement of faith), enumerated in the Constitution and Bylaws.

3. Distinct Ecclesiastical Government: Your church should have a distinct (officially adopted) ecclesiastical government in place. This is provided with bylaws.

4. Code of Doctrine and Discipline: Churches must have a systematic code of doctrine and discipline, including requirements for membership. Not having a written membership policy could be dangerous for a number of reasons:

   a. Your bylaws or some other official document must have enumerated the conditions of conduct under which a new member joins. If these are spelled out, the Church has the right to exercise discipline under the law. Without clear policy in force, any move to enact discipline would be interpreted as arbitrary and discriminatory. Please note: The Bible cannot be cited as the church's membership and discipline policy.

b. It is important to specify the procedure for discipline spelled out. The courts have rejected references to the Bible alone in themselves as insufficient rules for church discipline. Your interpretation of cited Biblical provisions must be spelled out so that some form of due process can be served.

5. Distinct Religious History: Your church's history must be preserved in some kind of written document, in order to demonstrate that it is not a "fly-by-night" operation.

6. Membership not associated with another church: Your church should maintain records substantiating that it has a membership not associated with another congregation. It is a good idea to develop some kind of system of keeping membership records, as well as a system of transferring the membership of persons who come from other churches to join yours. Even if the other churches do not respond (my pastoral experience is that most of them won't) you at least have a copy of the letter on file which indicates you tried.

7. Organization of ordained ministers: In your bylaws there should be stated rules and guidelines for other persons seeking ordination.

8. Ordained ministers serving after completing a prescribed course of study: A prescribed course of study gives credibility to ministerial credentials, and is almost always examined (not in content) by the IRS or the courts when questioning ministerial credentials.

9. Distinct literature: A church should have literature used in its operations. The Bible cannot be cited as "distinct literature" for these purposes.

10. Established place of worship: Your church should have an established place for public worship, although this may be a temporary rented facility.

11. Regular Congregation: Your church should have a constituency of persons regularly attending your church.

12. Regular Religious Services: Your church should offer regular services at stated times on a regular basis.

13. Sunday Schools and other training events: Your church should have a Sunday School or some other instruction for the young.

14. School for Ministerial Preparation: Your church should offer (or recommend) some form of Bible training for the preparation of ministers and lay workers.

While an exact number of these criteria has not been specified as necessary to establish church status, the IRS has generally stated that if an organization can demonstrate that it meets a majority of the fourteen points, it will be considered a church.[2]

In addition, the U. S. Tax Court ruled that while the fourteen-point list is helpful in determining the status of a church, it cannot be used as the sole determinative factor, and that many of the items listed are irrelevant to new churches.[3]

The IRS determinative test has been criticized by persons who specialize in church and law issues. Attorney Richard Hammar notes that the fourteen-point list is vague and seems to be directed to both local churches and denominational organizations. Hammar points out that the IRS does not indicate how many of the criteria an organization must meet to be classified a church, and if any of the criteria are more important than the others. Hammar further complains that the vagueness of the fourteen points means that "their application in any particular case will depend on the discretionary judgement of a government employee. This is the very kind of conduct that the courts repeatedly have condemned in other contexts as unconstitutional."[4]

It is interesting to note that the nineteen questions found in IRS Form 1023 Schedule A are designed to evaluate the applicant based on the fourteen-point test.

Endnotes

1. Richard Hammar, *Pastor Church and Law* (Matthews, North Carolina: Christian Ministry Resources, 1991), 248.

2. Ibid., 249.

3. Ibid., 250.

4. Ibid., 251-252.

ALSO AVAILABLE FROM HUNTINGTON HOUSE PUBLISHERS

- *ADD: ...the facts, ...the fables, ...hope for your family* — Theresa Lamson
- *Alzheimer's* — Teresa Strecker, Ph.D.
- *Anyone Can Homeschool* — Terry Dorian, Ph.D. & Zan Peters Tyler
- *The Basic Steps to Successful Homeschooling* — Vicki Brady
- *Beyond Political Correctness* — David Thibodaux, Ph.D.
- *Bible Promises for Little Ones* — Edited by David England
- *Big Book of Bible Promises* — Edited by David England
- *The Blame Game* — Lynn Stanley
- *Circle of Death* — Richmond Odom
- *Children No More* — Brenda Scott
- *Combat Ready* — Lynn Stanley
- *Conquering the Culture* — David Eich
- *The Cookbook* — Terry Dorian, Ph.D.
- *Dinosaurs and the Bible* — David Unfred
- *Do Angels Really Exist?* — Dr. David O. Dykes
- *Everyday Evangelism* — Ray Comfort
- *The First Lady: Hillary Rodham Clinton* — Peter & Timothy Flaherty
- *From Earthquakes to Global Unity* — Paul McGuire
- *The Gender Agenda* — Dale O'Leary
- *Global Bondage* — Cliff Kincaid
- *Global Taxes For A World Government* — Cliff Kincaid
- *Handouts and Pickpockets* — William Hoar
- *Health Begins in Him* — Terry Dorian, Ph.D.
- *Held By An Angel's Wings* — Raiea Hinson
- *High on Adventure I, II, & III* — Stephen Arrington
- *How to Homeschool (Yes, You!)* — Julia Toto
- *In His Majesty's Service* — Robert Peterson
- *A Jewish Conservative Looks at Pagan America* — Don Feder
- *Journey into Darkness* — Stephen Arrington
- *Legacy Builders* — Jim Burton
- *The Media Hates Conservatives* — Dale A. Berryhill
- *Out of Control* — Brenda Scott
- *Outcome-Based Education* — Peg Luksik & Pamela Hoffecker
- *To Grow By Storybook Readers* — Janet Friend
- *The Truth about False Memory Syndrome* — Dr. James Friesen

Available at bookstores everywhere or order direct from:

Huntington House Publishers
P.O. Box 53788 • Lafayette, LA 70505

Call toll-free 1-800-749-4009.